8/2021

Brian,

What a pleasure it was
you on the hiking trip
Can continue this Friendship "Fellow" cafe
eventually be a
enjoy the
read,
Hugs
Paul

By the
SEAT
of my
PANTS

By the SEAT of my PANTS

How I Survived a Nasty Divorce, an Incurable Disease, and Learned That No Matter How Bad Things Get, You Can Always Pay it Forward

CAROL CETRINO

ALLEN-CETRINO
ALPHARETTA, GA.

*The profits from the sale of this book after costs
will be donated to the Andrew C. Carlos MS Institute
at Shepherd Center in Atlanta.*

First Printing, 2014

Published by
Allen-Cetrino
Alpharetta, GA 30004

I dedicate this book to my son Ryan who was always my constant and my inspiration and to all the MS patients I have come to know because of their strength I have mine. I also want to thank God for putting the talented doctors, nurses and researchers within my reach and allowing me to have the quality of life I have been blessed with.

Contents

1

In the Beginning

'VE ALWAYS BEEN A FIGHTER.

Growing up poor on Long Island in a large, half-Italian half-Irish Catholic family with more comings and goings than Grand Central Station will tend to make you that way. At least if you want to survive your childhood, which I somehow managed to do, much to my own surprise. And the surprise of a lot of other people, too, come to think of it.

I was a little accident-prone, to say the least. By the time I was a teenager I'd had several concussions and too many cuts and bruises to count, more than I can remember. I was always falling down and hurting myself or running into things and knocking them over. My mother used to call me Calamity Jane because of all the havoc I wrought, but all of those incidents probably caused my father to give me a little extra attention, so it all evened out, I guess.

Everything happens for a reason.

I've often wondered if my disease was always there, lying dormant in the shadows, all those accidents explained away by my awkwardness, until it finally reared its ugly head in my twenties, when a lot of people are diagnosed with MS. Maybe I wasn't so clumsy after all. Maybe I already had symptoms.

Who knows? There's so much we don't know about multiple sclerosis today, let alone thirty years ago. I was diagnosed back in 1982, which was like the dark ages of the disease. There were no MRIs, no drug therapies, and no real tools with which to deal with the disease. Even so, there were plenty of people long before that who suffered much more than I did, I'm sure.

So I have to be grateful, I really do. For every hardship I've suffered, I can recount a blessing, as well. Life is all about your perspective. It's all in how you look at things.

Speaking of which, they say you are shaped by your family, so here's a little about my background. I would have to say that we were probably lower middle class more than we were actually poor, and maybe a little more Irish than Italian. I guess when I swear I'm Irish and when I drink I'm Italian, or maybe the other way around, but none of us kids had any idea we were poor or lower middle class or anything, really. We were mostly just like everybody else in the neighborhood. We didn't know rich from poor in those days. All we knew was what we saw.

My parents were in the same boat with most of our neighbors, struggling to make ends meet in order to live the American dream. You know, own a home, a car, have decent medical insurance, good schools, strive to give their kids more than they had. Or something like that. Sound familiar?

People in the neighborhood had barbecues, pool parties, and badminton. Everyone was welcome, and nothing was ever really planned. We all just showed up to have fun, and we did.

I suppose we were not as well off financially as some of the other families on the block, but that wasn't something I realized until I was older.

There were five of us kids and I was right in the middle, which helped make me the rebel of the family. I was young enough to get away with a few things my older brother and sister could resent me for, and old enough to ruin things just a little bit for my younger sisters. And because I was such a clumsy kid, my father was always extra protective of me. I was his darling, except when I wasn't, and believe me I tested his patience.

I was not a model child.

But I never got away with too much because my parents were tough. How could they not be, with five kids spread out over eleven years? I can't even imagine all the headaches we gave them. My father in particular was good at sniffing out whatever trouble I got myself into and making sure I was either too scared or too embarrassed to ever do it again, or at least to try harder not to get caught the next time. He was a prince of a man, my father, and still is. He would do anything for his children. Sometimes he worked three jobs to keep us all fed and clothed.

That said, you defied him at your own risk.

In those days my mother was a stay-at-home mom who tried to cope raising five kids with little money and no back–up. She didn't have any help from her parents, who lived in Florida and died shortly after I was born. My father's dad died shortly after my parents were married and his mother had to work. So there were no grandparents to help out like in a lot of families. Basically, my mother was on her own and did the best she could, which was probably made easier with a drink or two.

It was pretty difficult raising five kids with no money, so let's just say she was no Donna Reed, and had no desire to be, either. She was no cookie-cutter housewife, believe me. She definitely liked to drink and had her issues, but we didn't know it at the time. It wasn't like that was all she did. Everybody drank a lot in those days, at least in our neighborhood, and there was nothing unusual about it. All the parents had cocktails after work and beer on the weekends and nobody thought twice about it.

I have to sympathize with her, because being a stay-at-home mom with five children was no easy task. By the time we were all in school, she probably took one look at the mounds of laundry, stacks of dirty dishes, and unmade beds and it would have been pretty easy for cocktails to come a little earlier as time went by. It sounds overwhelming to me just to write about it.

In spite of all that, my mother was the one who really taught me to be a compassionate person. Growing up she might have been a little rough around the edges, but there's nothing that woman wouldn't do for someone who needs her help, and not just her family. I think she just took a while to find herself, as we often do. As abrupt and quick to judge as she can be, her heart is pure gold.

I remember a family had moved in down the block in one of the few rentals in the neighborhood. You could tell by the way they dressed and they way their house looked that they were very poor. I made friends with the little girl that lived there, and one day she invited me over to her house to play.

I couldn't believe how they lived; it was shocking. What little furniture they had was old and broken. When she opened the refrigerator to get some Kool-Aid, there was not much else there. I felt so bad for her that the next day I went into our pantry and took cans of tuna, beans, rice, and peanut butter and shoved it into a bag to take it to them.

My mom caught me on the way out and wanted to know what was in the bag, so I told her how poor the new people were and how they had no food.

"You know, Carol we don't have much either," she said.

"Well, we have way more than them."

My mother just looked at me for a moment and then grabbed the bag and stuffed some more things in it and handed it back to me. She never said another word. Although they only lived there for a short time, I continued to bring them groceries, and they were really appreciative.

When my baby sister Barbara Jean entered the second grade, she went to work at a local weight loss clinic doing intake. Which meant her job was to weigh the people when they first started the program. Whether that assignment made her want to drink even more, I couldn't say, but it might have pushed her in the general direction.

Her shift started at six in the evening, which was the time most other moms were home cooking dinner, or at least the Donna Reeds were, so you might say we didn't get all the motherly attention that some of the other kids in the neighborhood received. Frankly, we were fine with it. She wasn't the warmest of mothers, anyway, and by that time we were all pretty self-sufficient. We could fight like cats and dogs, but when it came down to it, we all looked out for each other.

Nobody really talked about those things, though, whether someone was an alcoholic or a neglectful parent. We didn't think that way because no one thought that way. It's not like we were abused or anything. Things were the way they were, and while it may not sound idyllic now, it was all we knew. We accepted things the way they were because we knew our parents loved us and would always be there for us, no matter what.

I'm sure there were plenty of other families in the neighborhood with their share of problems, too. Nobody's perfect. As a kid, things don't always make sense until you look back with a little perspective.

When I compare the old neighborhood to how things are today, I have to say I had a pretty great childhood and I wouldn't trade it for anything. We played running bases or stick ball or hide and seek out in the street until dusk, went inside for dinner, and did it all again the next day. It was a different time, and no one worried about abuse or abductions; as long as we were in shouting distance of our parents, no one worried. The neighborhood was filled with kids, and there was always something to do.

My parents have been divorced now for forty years, and I love them both more than I can say. They're as different as night and day and always have been, but deep down I know they care for each other and always will. All those years together and five children, how else could they be?

For a long time my father never really had steady employment. He worked odd jobs, basically whatever he could find, from demolition work on construction sites to plowing snow on the runways at JFK to bartending to delivering oil to selling appliances to whatever else he could find. I used to love watching him knock down buildings with heavy machinery. There's just something about the power to destroy that really makes a girl swoon, I guess, especially when it's her father.

When I was around sixteen he got on with the Teamsters, which made things a little easier in terms of finances, but there were a lot of lean years before that.

He'd come home after a long day and make sure the kids were all fed and our homework was done, (at least we told him it was done) and took us wherever we needed to go, basically doing whatever needed to be done. When my mother took the night job it meant my dad had even more responsibility, which he never seemed to mind.

I don't think it bothered him a bit that she wasn't around to do a lot of the things mothers typically do because he really seemed to enjoy his kids.

My mom was not all that good at handling us, anyway. She doesn't like a lot of commotion unless it's hers, and that's all we were sometimes. Mom always had that look in her eyes like she'd rather be on a desert island or in a library or almost anyplace quieter than a houseful of noisy kids. Looking back, I feel sorry for her. She really had no idea what she was getting into.

I'll never forget the time I told her I volunteered her for cookie mother with my Girl Scout troop. I was the only one of us kids who did stuff like that. Her jaw dropped and she looked at me like I was from another planet.

"Are you out of your mind?"

My mother can be very imperious-sounding, and does not suffer fools gladly. She's a very intelligent woman and she expects everyone around her to know what she knows and understand what she understands, whether you're in the fourth grade or you're eighty-seven, and she's never afraid of telling you what's on her mind.

Her opinions are never a secret.

"I can't be a cookie-mother!" She said incredulously.

From her lips, "cookie-mother" sounded horrific, as if I'd asked her to mate with the Creature from the Black Lagoon.

"Get the hell out of here!"

I was eight.

I love my mother, but tact was not her strong suit. In terms of conversations, she likes to begin them if possible and end them absolutely. I think she believes the last word should always be hers because she's right, which I have to admit, is often the case.

And the telephone? Forget about it. She hates wasting time on the phone. She says her piece and then hangs up as quickly as she can. Very abrupt, my mother.

Come to think of it, that probably describes most of her face-to-face conversations, too. Most people have never been hung up on when they're not even on the phone, but most people have never met my mother.

On my parents' 26th wedding anniversary, all of us kids pooled our money together to give them a party. We all worked to help out with family finances, but even so it wasn't a very large pool.

My older sister Janet, who inherited my mother's direct way of speaking, eventually got frustrated and blurted out, "I don't know why we're even bothering, they're just going to get divorced!"

I was shocked. At sixteen, I knew kids with divorced parents, but I had never even considered my own parents might split up. Stuff like that happened to other people.

It was a scary thought.

"I don't know what you're talking about!" I said defiantly.

"Carol, they fight all the time."

"So?" I knew for a fact a lot of parents argued.

"Mother's an alcoholic and Daddy can't stand it!"

Her words were like a slap in the face. I needed a comeback.

"Then why are they together?"

I had her now. Irrefutable logic wins the day.

Janet rolled her eyes in that irritating, older sister way. "Because we're poor!" She answered. "Where they gonna go with no money?"

No comeback for that one.

Janet went back to counting our meager savings, completely unaware that she'd totally rocked my world. My big sister Janet was always brutally honest, sometimes too brutal.

I tried to act like it was no big deal, but I was really devastated.

First of all, I had no idea our mother was an alcoholic, and second, I had no idea we were living in poverty. What a wake-up call that was!

Everybody's parents drank as far as I knew. We lived in a nice house. Maybe it wasn't as nice as the other houses in the neighborhood, and maybe other dads had nicer cars, and maybe there were a few bottles around … but like I said, it wasn't much different from the rest of the neighborhood.

I have to laugh at how clueless I was. Ignorance is bliss, all right. My entire childhood would have been completely different had I known what was actually going on around me.

Suddenly it all made sense, and I knew Janet was right. Now I could see things clearly. The scales had fallen from my eyes and I had seen the light, like Paul on the road Damascus. Our parents were on the verge of a nasty divorce and we were destined for the poorhouse, and all it took was my know-it-all older sister to set me straight.

Of course, it wasn't quite as bad as all that. My imagination was in overdrive.

Eventually they did split up, but their divorce was not all that nasty because they finally were in agreement about something. They both knew they wanted to be away from each other. And none of us went to the poorhouse since we all learned to work from an early age. Lazy children, our parents did not raise.

I started working when I was twelve, hustling packages outside the grocery store for tips, and then as a mother's helper at the beach club in the summertime.

Many of the wealthy families I worked for on Long Island belonged to really nice beach clubs, a lot of which are still there. The clubs all had cabanas and restaurants and pools, and of course there was the beach. They were wonderful.

The mothers were there to see their friends, so they hired kids like me to watch their children for a few hours every afternoon in the summer, which was a great job.

I basically got paid thirty dollars a week to hang out at the beach, which was a lot of money back then. I worked for one family with two young children, who were never any trouble because they just wanted to build sand castles and play with their friends. Plus, I would usually babysit them on Friday and Saturday nights, so I kept pretty busy.

I also babysat for other families, sold donuts and pizza by the slice, basically anything for a few bucks. Looking back, I guess I was kind of like my father in that regard, taking whatever job I could find. We all did, expect for the youngest, Barbara Jean. She never worked all that much while growing up like the rest of us older kids. She was the baby of the family and so we all spoiled her. We wanted her to have a nice childhood.

Our parents bought us the basic necessities, but if we wanted certain things like a better pair of sneakers, or my favorite shampoo (Herbal Essence) or some cereal we'd seen on TV, that was on us. A lot of the things other parents bought for their kids we had to buy for ourselves.

I did all that for about four years until I turned sixteen and could get a regular job. To be honest, I was eager to get out on my own as soon as possible. The way I saw it, the age of eighteen was when you left home. Living in a very small house with seven people and one bathroom was not my idea of paradise. I can't imagine what my father and brother dealt with, having to share with five females. There were lots of times you'd have to go next door if someone was taking too long. When you gotta go, you gotta go.

The Willises and the Rohrs were pretty cool about it because they had kids we hung out with, but God help you if you knocked on the Rizzos' door because they were extremely uptight.

My father even issued an edict that no shower could be longer than seven minutes, a rule I was constantly getting yelled at for breaking. That's one of the reasons I love taking long, hot baths, because that was a luxury I did not enjoy growing up.

When you use your neighbor's bathroom, you get to know them pretty well, so I also got in the habit of going to them for other things. I don't know how many times I ran across the street to Mrs. Mundinger's and told her that my mother sent me over because she'd "forgotten" to pick up some snacks at the grocery store for our lunches that day, which of course was untrue. Our mother didn't even buy snacks for our lunches, at least nothing we actually wanted to eat.

"Of course, dear," Mrs. Mundinger would say, and go to the kitchen and bring out something good for all of us to put in the lunches we took to school every day. I thought I was being so sneaky, but I'm sure she knew what was going on.

Kids always think they're getting away with a lot more than they are. Most of the time the adults are too nice or too busy to correct them.

Mrs. Mundinger was one of the nice ones.

On the weekends the cool thing to do was hang out at C&J's Bowling Alley, which we all did, of course. I was not a good bowler, but I was fun in other ways. I'd go over to my friends' houses and listen to the Beatles or the Supremes, watch Dark Shadows and talk about boys or how much school sucked. Life was good.

I never wanted to follow the rules, and so I left that for others to worry about. That attitude was just one of the reasons I had so many knockdown, drag-out fights with my older sister.

Janet always had to be perfect, probably because she was the eldest child and was always told to "set an example" for the rest of us. I think she resented the pressure, and I can't say that I blame her, but that goody two-shoes stuff wasn't for me, no way. We were constantly at each other's throats about it.

"Look Janet, I cook dinner when I'm supposed to, I work, I give money - "

"When things are tough, you disappear!"

"You want to hang around and do all that other crap, be my guest!"

"It's not crap!"

"You're not my mother!"

That made her crazy when I said that, because it was true. She wasn't my mother. She was just supposed to act like it when needed. Janet and I argued constantly as teenagers because of that, but now we're very close. I never realized how much it hurt her to hear me say some of those things, especially the mother thing, until I was married and had a child of my own. Because Janet really did a lot for our family that I didn't appreciate at the time. As I've said, our mother just wasn't all that into the whole "raising kids" thing, so Janet picked up a lot of the slack in that regard. She was like the assistant manager of a department store who got stuck with all the dirty jobs because the manager was messing around somewhere else.

Janet was the assistant mother.

She was also right. I was a hard worker, but very irresponsible. And I did disappear when things were tough, or sometimes even when they weren't. I was headstrong, wild, and a little fearless, and I would get these crazy ideas in my head and act on them without a thought for the consequences.

A good example of this was when I was sixteen. My best friend Laura and I hitchhiked to Kentucky because I thought it would be cool to see Appalachia. Seriously. Also, Laura had a boyfriend there, so she was anxious to go see him. But had I not been so eager to go, I doubt we would have made the trip.

Mike had dropped out of school and gone to work after his parents died in a car accident. He'd been left with nothing, but he led what two young girls thought was an exciting life, being on his own and not much older than we were.

We got in a lot of trouble for that little trip. My father had the cops in three states looking for me when he got my postcard from Knoxville that said everything was fine and I would "be home soon."

After that, it was fifteen states.

Laura was a rebel like me, a very smart girl who didn't care much for rules. Her father was dead and her mother was an alcoholic, so she was also a little wild, which made us a really good match and a really terrible combination.

We took what money we had at the time and just went out to the interstate and stuck out our thumbs. That was the extent of our planning. We got a ride right away from the first of several truckers, which sounds really scary today, I know. But we were both small and kind of waifish looking, not curvy at all, and I think the men all felt more protective of us that anything else.

We looked like little girls, really, and most of the people who picked us up would tell us they had a daughter like us at home, and give us money and really try to help us out. They were mostly aghast that we were out hitchhiking, actually, so we made up stories that we were on our way home instead of the other way around, which seemed to make them feel a lot better.

I can't believe we were such good little liars.

At first it was great. It felt like an adventure, and it was. But adventures go better with money, and when our money ran out it was a lot less fun, and it ran out pretty fast. Then we got caught in a terrible rainstorm, which was awful for us but at least made us look even more pathetic, which garnered more sympathy. But after a few hours of that, we were muddy and cranky and eager to get somewhere with a nice bed and a bathroom.

Me, in particular. I was always fanatical about my hair, even more than your typical teenage girl, and most of my knapsack was taken up with what I needed for hair maintenance, like my hairdryer, shampoo, and conditioner. There was also peanut butter and marijuana, of course.

Like I said, ours was not a well-planned trip.

I would actually blow dry my hair in the nasty truck stop bathrooms, if you can believe that.

We were down to coins when we finally got to Mike's place, and he was pretty surprised to see us, to say the least. Downright stupefied, he was.

Laura had told him she was coming, or so I thought, but even if he got her letter he probably never thought she'd actually show up. With a friend, no less.

Not only that, he was living with his girlfriend, the one he never told her about, and so we couldn't even stay with him!

Imagine the situation. Two cold, wet, hungry teenage girls without two nickels between them, looking forward to finally sleeping in a bed, or at least on a friendly couch, and suddenly we realize we had just hitchhiked our way into homelessness.

Those smelly truck cabs were sounding really good at that moment.

Mike, who was working as a cook in a mental hospital, which I guess was good preparation for our visit, called a friend who said we could stay with her for a few days. That made us very happy until we actually saw her apartment, which was like something out of a horror movie.

A hovel would have been a major improvement. It was literally the worst place I'd ever seen.

I had just gotten to the age when I realized I was actually poor, but looking at this girl and how she lived, I felt like a Rockefeller.

Mike's friend lived in one tiny room. We walked in and just looked around like we'd stumbled onto some alien landscape. Neither of us had ever seen anything like it.

There was a single bed, a lamp, a window with ratty curtains, and that was it for furnishings. In the middle of what she called the kitchen, I kid you not, was a toilet.

There was a plastic curtain that could be pulled around the commode, and we both realized, to our dismay, that it was where she sat to take a shower.

On the toilet. In the middle of the kitchen.

Ever heard the expression, "you don't shit where you eat"?

Theoretically, I suppose you could sit down and do your business while you scrambled eggs and took a shower. It was, as Frank Zappa would say a few years later, grody to the max!

That poor girl could literally take care of all her bodily functions without moving more than three feet in any direction.

Suddenly I didn't feel so poor anymore.

What's even worse, the place was not sparkling clean, either. To be honest, it was disgusting. I do a lot of volunteer work now, and I've met a lot of disadvantaged people. People who are extremely poor, but the memory of that girl's apartment has stayed with me all these years.

It was very cold that night, so the three of us all crowded into the same little bed as Laura and I tried not to imagine how long it had been since the sheets were washed. But I was so tired I drifted off pretty quickly, in spite of the accommodations.

I woke up just as fast to one of the oddest conversations I'd ever heard in my life up to that point.

"Don't touch me there!" Laura barked.

"Don't be so frigid!" Replied the dungeon master.

Oh my God, what was happening now?

I didn't even know what frigid meant. All I knew was that Laura had some sort of problem with Elvira, Mistress of the Dark.

"What's going on?" I whispered.

"Carol, she's a lesbian and she's making moves on me," Laura said, matter-of-factly.

She was a little bit more experienced than me, sexually speaking.

"Oh my God, are you serious?" I asked.

"You sleep next to her."

"I'm not sleeping next to her!"

"I can hear what you're saying. I'm right here," said Elvira.

Needless to say, we left her right then and there, alone in her creepy little bed, and moved on.

That's when I sent the postcard to my father.

I regret putting him through all that nonsense when I was a kid. My mother, too, but it seemed to hit my father a little bit harder sometimes.

He'd always had a soft spot for me because of my physical problems. I was a small girl, always bumping into things and falling down, which of course we all just thought was me being a klutz, and Daddy called me his little Princess. Janet was just plain old Janet.

That may have had something to do with our arguments, too.

It really wasn't my fault, though. Janet just developed more quickly. It didn't hurt that she worked at Friendly's scooping ice cream, which really builds the biceps. Janet had muscles on her muscles.

Janet was one tough girl, and still is.

I, on the other hand, was always the small, scrappy one, which is why my father was always so gentle with me. And remember, I was always the one getting hurt.

My first major accident was when I was four. It is a memory I will never forget, and probably neither will anyone else in my family. It was pretty traumatic for all of us.

Actually, my father wasn't at home the day I crashed through the glass storm door, nicking an artery and bleeding all over the house like a stuck pig, but he saw the aftermath in the hospital, and it was not pretty.

I vividly remember running around the house playing while Q-tip, our dog that my mother hated, was barking outside. Mother was busy changing the baby, my little sister Joanne, and yelled for me to close the front door, because if the door wasn't latched Q-tip could push his way in.

I ran toward the door and tripped, smashing into the glass, which shattered. I fell through the jagged opening onto the porch, cutting my wrist and gouging that artery.

Screaming from fear as much as anything else, I ran into the bedroom where my little sister was still gurgling on the bed. My mother took one look at the fountain of blood squirting from my arm and passed out.

That scared me even more, so I ran out the back door, screaming.

Thank God a neighbor saw me in the driveway, because otherwise I probably would have bled to death right there.

Franny was a bartender who lived down the street, a nice man with twelve kids. He took one look at me and went as white as a sheet, but fortunately did not pass out. He ran over and scooped me into his arms and drove me to the hospital, somehow holding onto my arm to at least slow the bleeding.

Franny the bartender saved my life.

It took two hundred stitches to close the wound, and I was in the hospital for two weeks, which was an eternity for a kid my age. I think my father blamed my mother for what happened, and while it wasn't her fault, I know she felt pretty bad about it. It was actually a very traumatic experience for them both, and caused a lot of stress in their marriage, which they certainly didn't need.

Living in a tiny house with five kids was stressful enough even if they behaved themselves, which we certainly didn't. Looking back on it, I'm surprised their marriage lasted as long as it did.

My parents were two very passionate people who loved each other but couldn't stand each other, who fought a lot but always made up, who never got physical but left plenty of scars. They argued just as passionately as they made children.

I'm sure they had a loud one after I crashed through that door.

It made things harder, not only in their relationship, but for our entire family. I had to be watched carefully after that, and with a newborn in the house it was more work for everyone. That's another thing Janet had to do that I never realized until much later. Plus, I was still every bit as rambunctious after my hospital stay, just like any typical preschooler.

I was pretty fearless as a child, which probably helped prepare me for my life as an adult with MS. As I said, I truly believe everything happens for a reason, and whatever I went through as a kid happened to better prepare me for the future.

The incident with the door wasn't the end of my injuries, either. It was the beginning. I really learned to live up to my nickname after that. The floodgates opened like that fountain of blood from my artery, and it was one thing after another with me, it seemed.

There was the incident when I fell off a swing, stood up, and got dinged in the head by the metal seat, then got hit again as the swing made another pass! That was my first concussion. I was like a walking Three Stooges routine. All I needed were the sound effects.

There was always something going on with Daddy's little princess.

Years later when I got back home from that trip to Kentucky, my parents sent me to a psychiatrist, who told them I was very smart and adventuresome and not at all unstable.

"Tell me something I don't know," my mother replied.

"Then what's the matter with her?" My father asked.

"She's also very bored."

Which was true. I never studied much after I switched from Catholic school to public school in the 8th grade. I just didn't want to bother with it all. I was in a rush to grow up and see the world.

"She's not a drug addict," the psychiatrist continued. "She's not doing this because she hates you, or because she hates herself, or because she hates anything. She's just...looking for new adventures."

"Adventures?" My dad repeated.

"Adventures," said the psychiatrist. "She needs to be challenged."

My father just shook his head.

"And she's bored."

"Bored?".

The psychiatrist nodded.

It was true, all of it. I was bored, I was looking for adventure, and I definitely wanted to be challenged.

Be careful what you wish for.

"Sometimes you just have to let kids find themselves."

My father looked dubious.

"Mister Cetrino, there is no formula," she said. "Half the time we're all just flying by the seat of our pants."

If that's not the story of my life, I don't know what is.

2

Nunsense

I WAS A GOOD KID UNTIL THE 9TH GRADE, BECAUSE IF you stepped out of line in Catholic school the nuns would really beat the crap out of you, at least they did back in the sixties and early seventies when I was there.

That's not to say that was a bad thing, quite the contrary. I needed the discipline, whether I realized it or not. It wasn't what I wanted, but it was just what I needed.

Which reminds me of an old joke:

How many kids in catholic school understand they need structure and discipline?

The answer is nun.

I highly recommend sending your kids to Catholic school if at all possible, even if you're not Catholic. It's like the Marines, only with Bible verses. If every kid in America got a Catholic school education, I really believe we'd be a lot better off. And it's not even the religion, although that's there, of course. It's the discipline. The rules you have to follow. In too many public schools, the rules are not enforced and so the kids just learn that they can defy authority.

I sent my own son to catholic high school and believe me, it made all the difference. He is the most polite, responsible, and compassionate kid you'd ever want to meet. And I believe a large part of it was because we attended church regularly and he went to a Catholic high school. All of our friends in the neighborhood went to the same church, which was also a big influence. It was something we all enjoyed doing, and it was something we could count on. It made us closer friends and better neighbors.

I went to a Catholic school from the first to the eighth grades, and it was an experience I'll never forget.

My grades were really good all the way through the 8th grade, too. My study habits were good, everything was very controlled, and even though I was never one for rules, I responded very well to the structure.

I was not yet the little hellion I turned into as soon as I became a teenager.

The sisters at my school were very tough, and while I may have gotten in trouble on more than one occasion, it was all small stuff. I didn't get into any major trouble until I transferred to public high school, which was when all hell broke loose.

We wore the uniforms, of course, and just wearing the clothes gives you a kind of regimented feeling. I'm all for individuality, but the uniforms make sense to me. As a kid it made you feel part of the group. Kids need to feel like they belong, and I even think there was less bullying as a result, although that stuff will always exist among kids.

It's a lot harder to tell who's rich and who's poor and who's different when everyone dresses alike. It was harder to single you out. Plus, if anyone was going to single you out for abuse, it was much more likely to be one of the sisters than another student. We did not really have the same kind of bullying we have today.

Kids will be kids, though, and if the group wanted to find a way to ostracize you, they could find a way. There's not much in the way of cruelty that kids won't discover on their own, I suppose. And not much the good Lord is going to do about human nature. After all, that's how He created us.

It was just easier to keep us kids in line in Catholic school, I think. It's really hard to misbehave too badly in front of a nun. Even today, whenever I see a nun or a priest, I'm automatically on my best behavior, and I think even non-Catholics are like that. There's just something about the uniform. It's like when you're at a stoplight and a cop pulls up beside you. Suddenly you're aware of every little thing you're doing that could even be construed as breaking the law.

Even so, I could still find ways to rebel. It's like the scorpion and the frog. It's my nature.

Sometimes it even happened by accident.

I'll never forget the time when I had to go to the bathroom really, really bad. That bursting bladder had quite an impact, not only on me, but the entire school.

Of course, there was a time for going to the bathroom just like there was a time for everything else, and in the middle of a lesson with Sister Mary Francis was not that time.

Sister Mary Francis was one of those nuns you've all heard about if not actually experienced, who was universally feared by the entire student body. Her reputation not only preceded her actual presence, but could actually haunt you. She was old and mean and completely unyielding in her interpretation of the rules. Rules were not meant to be broken in her view, and she was more than willing to persuade you of that with a swift ruler or a hard knuckle.

She looked like the actress who would play her in the movies, only ten times scarier. You did not mess with Sister Mary Francis.

We called her Sister Mary Frankenstein behind her back, and there were kids who swore they'd seen the bolts in her neck when she adjusted her habit on warm spring days.

I think she may have known that and been secretly flattered, but it's just a guess. She did almost seem to enjoy making small children quake as she passed, knowing our frightened little eyes would be less likely to stray from our lessons while she walked the earth.

Even some of the other nuns seemed a little afraid of her, to tell you the truth, and if Sister Mary Frankenstein was in the vicinity, there would be no mercy offered by even the nicer nuns to even the most harmless malfeasance. I would not have been at all surprised to learn that the Holy Father himself watched his step in her presence.

Until the day of the miraculous pee.

I was nine years old and sitting in Sister Mary Francis' class when the sudden and overwhelming urge to go came over me. I had foolishly not made time before her class, thinking I could last until the next break, but I immediately understood that was just not happening. Sometimes you can hold it and sometimes you can't, and this was definitely one of the latter times, and I knew it.

One of the other sisters might have taken pity on me, but not Sister Mary Frankenstein. I closed my eyes really tightly and held them that way for a moment before opening them.

I looked at the clock.

Twenty-seven minutes. Maybe I could do it if I tried really, really hard.

I crossed my legs, fidgeting in my seat. I couldn't possibly even raise my hand to ask because I knew what she'd say. I had to find some way to hold it in.

I closed my eyes again and uttered a silent prayer.

I looked at the clock.

Twenty-seven minutes? How could it still be twenty-seven minutes until the break? It was twenty-seven minutes almost ten minutes ago! I'll never make it.

I clenched, shutting my eyes so tightly I could see stars. I figured if I kept my eyes closed for a good, long while, the time would go by faster and when I opened them I'd be surprised.

"Carol Cetrino!"

I opened my eyes and sat up straight.

"Are you sleeping in my class?"

"No, Sister!"

Her eyes narrowed as Sister Mary Frankenstein considered whether to exact punishment on me. I almost hoped she would.

Maybe she'll send me to the principal's office!

She turned her attention from me and went back to the lesson. I uncrossed and crossed my legs again and finally allowed myself to look up at the clock.

Twenty-seven minutes?! How was that possible?

My hand shot up. I didn't even wait for Sister Mary Frankenstein to call on me, I just blurted out the words with the force of a hurricane.

"Can I go to the bathroom please?"

Sister Mary Francis looked at me, aghast that I'd interrupted her. The entire class went silent. Nobody interrupted Sister Mary Frankenstein, and nobody was allowed to go to the bathroom during her class. For a moment she just stared at me like my mom when I asked her to be the cookie mother.

"Absolutely not! You will wait until class is over and you will - "

"I have to gooooooooooo!" I wailed, standing up and moving from side to side. I thought I was going to pee all over myself at any moment. It was excruciating.

"Young lady, sit down this instant!" Sister Mary Frankenstein looked very angry, and a little confused. She was not used to anyone, least of all a third grader, hesitating to follow her commands.

I was in so much pain I was nearly crying. I started to sit, but as soon as I began to squat I felt the first tiny little drop squeeze itself out, which meant there was no stopping it if I didn't do something fast. I could either sit down and quietly pee all over my chair, or run for the door and pray Sister Mary Frankenstein didn't catch me as I flew past her.

I went for the door.

"Ahhhhhhhhhhhhhhhhhhhhhhhh I have to gooooooooooooo!" I screamed, and ran as fast as I could toward the door. I felt the Sister's fingers in my hair as I slammed into the door, throwing it aside even as I felt the sweet release of warm pee all the way down the hall, and my legs.

By the time I got to the girls' bathroom there was nothing left, so I just kept running, out the door of the school and down the street, fueled by shame and fear and self-loathing.

Agony never felt so good.

I ran all the way home, wet with urine and wet with tears, bursting into the house just as my mother was pouring herself another cocktail.

"Carol - "

I ran into my room and slammed the door, waiting for my punishment. Surely I could not escape the wrath of Sister Mary Frankenstein and my mother.

But when she came in, my mother was gentle and kind and understanding. She could tell I was in mortal peril. She told me to take a nice hot shower and change clothes, and she called my father.

I was even allowed to stay in there longer than seven minutes!

I was so worried I might get in trouble or it would somehow cause an argument, but both of my parents were really nice to me, and to each other. They may have fought like cats and dogs sometimes, but when it came to their children, they were together. Especially in times of trouble.

Now, peeing down your leg in the third grade is not exactly the Great Depression or anything, but it was a very big deal to me and they recognized that. Little traumas can scar a kid for life if you don't handle them right.

My parents did.

The next day I stayed home from school and my mother took me shopping while my father went to the school. I had no idea what was going to happen, but everyone was being so sweet to me I didn't care. Time alone with my mother was rare in a house with five kids, and it felt good. She was much better with us one on one. And I had no doubt my father would fix things, somehow.

Like I said, the man did what needed to be done.

I was eating ice cream with my mother when my dad walked into the house just before lunchtime and called me over to sit on his lap.

"How you doing, Princess?"

I smiled. Whatever worry I had about what transpired between my father and the nuns was gone.

"I'm fine, Daddy."

He leaned his face into mine and looked deeply into my eyes. There was always such kindness in my father's eyes. Even today, I see the same thing when I look at him, which I don't get to do nearly enough.

I love to look in my father's eyes.

"You're going back to school tomorrow. And from now on, you go to the bathroom whenever you want. Understand?"

My eyes grew wide. "Are you sure?" I was thinking about Sister Mary Frankenstein.

He nodded. "And that goes for every other kid, too."

I couldn't believe it. My daddy had vanquished Sister Mary Frankenstein. He was a hero. My hero.

The next day, however, it was me who was the hero. I had been so scared the other kids would tease me about peeing all over myself, but instead I was the kid who got the rules changed. Sister Mary Frankenstein's rules.

Bathroom breaks for everyone!

Sister Mary Francis never said a word about how I'd disobeyed her, either. As a matter of fact, she acted as if the whole thing had never happened. She was almost, dare I say, nice to me the next day. After that, I never looked at her the same way again. She wasn't so scary anymore. She was a nun and my teacher, not a Frankenstein.

I liked her a lot better after that.

Overall, it had been a great experience after the initial horror. Time with my mother, my dad the hero, my parents getting along. What more could a girl ask for?

I have no idea at all what my father said to the nuns at my school, and he barely even remembers it now, but that was one of the most memorable events of my childhood.

It's funny how we remember things. My mother and father were just doing their job as parents, doing what needed to be done for their daughter, never realizing how much that day meant to me as a kid.

Living with MS, you learn there are good days and bad days, but every day is a blessing.

The day I peed myself, united my parents, and turned Frankenstein human?

That was a good day.

3

Moving On

I CAN'T STRESS ENOUGH HOW MUCH OF A CULTURE shock it was for me when I graduated from Catholic school and transferred into a public junior high for the ninth grade.

Everything had been so regimented for me before, with the uniforms and the discipline, so when all of that was taken away in one fell swoop, it was quite the life changer for a kid my age.

With the sisters in charge, you did what you were told when you were told to do it, in spite of my bathroom break victory. You were in a line most of the time if you weren't sitting in class, and if you messed up they would force you up against the wall, literally. At recess you would actually have to stand with your face to the wall for the entire period, and it was elevated so everyone on the playground could see you. That was the punishment for running.

Running at recess.

One thing about rules, though. If you're a typical kid, rules are things you want to break. Rules are boundaries, and boundaries are crossed. Standing with your face to the wall where everyone could see you was not a deterrent to me except to try harder the next time not to get caught.

But as soon as the uniform was no longer required and there were no nuns watching every move I made, it was like the liberation of Paris after the war. I divided my life as before my freedom and after, and I went a little crazy.

I was just so astounded that suddenly I could do whatever I wanted and nobody cared, although it only seemed like that, of course. Even for the time, my transgressions were not all that serious. It as really pretty typical kid stuff.

Up to that point, my childhood had been innocent and idyllic, and now a whole new world had opened up for me.

As a rebellious kid, I naturally gravitated to others of like mind. I was a fun kid, and I looked for girlfriends who shared my sensibility. We rolled up our skirts, which was a way of rebelling against the uniforms, we wore mascara when we could get away with it, which was a way to express our budding sexuality, and we basically kept looking for boundaries even as they started to slowly fall away. This was the late sixties and the early seventies, which was a tumultuous and fascinating time to come of age.

We screamed for the Monkees, rushed home after school to watch TV, and began to smoke and drink just like our parents did. What we wanted to do was grow up, and I was an anxious as any of my friends to do so. I couldn't wait to get out of the house and travel and make my mark on the world.

My father, however, as all fathers, was in no such hurry.

My father was a tough man. As I said, he would do just about anything for his family, but he was no pushover. He may have been a big softie inside, but he could also be just as scary as Sister Mary

Frankenstein when he wanted to be. You did not cross my father without consequences.

I remember we had one of those above ground pools for a while when I was younger, and my father was constantly telling us kids we had to take care of it. We were supposed to keep it filled in the summer and make sure the water was clean, and keep the yard down around it since he was so busy working.

"You kids better take care of that damn thing or I'll take it away," he'd say, more times than we could count.

Sure enough, one spring when we had been particularly negligent in our duties, we came home from school and not only was the pool completely gone, but most of the yard had been bricked over like a patio.

My father did not make idle threats.

A few days later we were all out of school for the summer, wishing we had taken him seriously.

Once I was in high school, I kicked my adventurous side up a notch and my scholastic side was pushed to the back burner. Aside from the lessons I got from that little hitchhiking excursion, I also learned to blow the perfect smoke ring, roll a joint with a dollar bill, and make a pipe from a tampon. I wore the tightest jeans I could find, using a coat hanger to zip them up, skipped school with my friends, and basically stopped studying unless I absolutely had to.

While the neighborhood parents were all playing cards and getting loaded, the kids were all cruising and getting high. I could tie-dye the perfect psychedelic shirt and pierce my friends' ears with a needle and an ice cube, and I was having the time of my life.

I hid my Yodels in the freezer so my sisters wouldn't eat them and the good underwear in the encyclopedia so my sisters couldn't wear them. In a house full of teenage girls, everyone shared clothes and you had to be tricky to get what you wanted.

My sister Janet went so far as to put a padlock on her bedroom door because she was so tired of me wearing her clothes, but I just took the door off the hinges and got them, anyway.

For years I remembered this story the other way, that it was I who was forced to lock away my things from my sisters, but when I began preparations for this book it was brought to my attention that I was the thief and not the victim, at least that time.

Regardless, when my father came home from work he had two daughters at each other's throats over underwear and a couple of hinges, so he just sighed and put the door back the way it was supposed to be and then removed the padlock for good, which was as close to Solomon as he could have gotten with the two of us.

I also used work to separate myself from home, taking a job as TSS, or Times Square Stores, as soon as I turned sixteen. I worked the coffee counter, pouring coffee and serving donuts, but I bopped around a lot, going from job to job depending on how much money I could make.

Janet, being the solid citizen that she was, stayed at Friendly's all through high school, and my brother Tom, who was as smart as a whip, managed to remain studious all through school and worked at a refrigeration company. That was his first real job and put him through college.

Even our younger sister Joanne was more stable than me as far as employment was concerned, working at Burger King all through high school.

It's not that I was not a good worker; on the contrary, I was an excellent employee. I worked really hard no matter what the job and always took it seriously, it was just that I had that wanderlust in my heart. I was always looking for something better, something different, and if that meant switching jobs, that was fine by me.

Deep down, I guess I was unsettled. It was like the psychiatrist told my parents, I got bored easily.

Even today, I like to fill my time with new things. I may not have been a good student, but I was a terrific learner.

One of the best jobs I had was working for this crazy old woman who founded a chain of bagel shops with her husband. Once he died, her ungrateful children didn't really treat her very well, and I worked as her aide after her daughter put her in a nursing home.

Ada was a real handful because, like I said, she was a little nuts, and eventually the nursing home director insisted her kids hire someone to kin of babysit her in the nursing home, which I thought was strange because what are they being paid for?

That requirement, however, got me the job as her minder, and I had a blast.

Ada and I got along really well because we were both straight shooters. She would say the most outrageous things and I wouldn't bat an eye, and we both made each other laugh. She needed a laugh after being in that crappy nursing home, too.

I worked for her five days a week for about a year, but it was a little tough in the beginning. The first time I saw her, I thought I would die.

Her fingernails were long and curled, with disgusting gunk in them like they hadn't been cleaned for decades. It was horrible. I got her all cleaned up, but I found out later that her daughter had kept Ada locked away in a room in her house for years, which may have contributed to her condition.

I mean, did she go crazy because she was locked away or was she locked away because she was crazy?

But I loved Ada, and once we got to know each other, we got along quite well. She would say the most outrageous things to total strangers. If we met someone while we were out and about, she would always introduce herself, spell her name, and tell the person that her kids were bums. She was a real character.

I made sure she showered and brushed her teeth, took her to doctors appointments, read to her, took her out to lunch, we walked on the boardwalk. I even took her to baseball games and to my parents' house a few times, anything to get her out of that hellhole her children were paying for.

I really developed a healthy respect for old people during that year, seeing how Ada was treated. No one should live like that, no matter who they are. I can't imagine how bleak her life would have been if her kids didn't have the means to hire someone to take care of her in addition to the nursing home staff, who were caretakers only in the loosest sense of the word.

That experience really made an impression on me, and today whenever I come across elderly people who are alone or without help, I go out of my way to reach out to them, even if it's just to say hello and chat for a bit. I think it meant a lot to Ada and I know it would mean a lot to me if I was in that situation.

Meanwhile, I had been doing absolutely nothing in school. As soon as I got into high school, all hell broke loose. I wasn't studying; I was getting high every day and ditching classes, basically doing everything wrong.

I was having a great time.

In the tenth grade I got suspended and my father had to come to the school to get me, which he was not at all happy about. I'll never forget when he said, "Let's go to your locker and get your books," and I had to admit to him that I had no locker.

"Where do you keep your books?" He demanded.

"Uh…I don't have any books," I stammered.

Which was true. I was really just skating through, not caring about anything. I was smart enough to pass my classes and that was about it.

My father was completely shocked. It must have been awful for him. First of all, he had to drop everything and leave work to come down and get me, and then he was standing face to face with his little girl, his princess, and she was a total mess.

He looked at me like I was an alien being, and then he slammed his fist into a locker (not mine, of course) and scared the living hell out of me. I don't think I've ever seen him so mad. It was really the only time he just lost it with me.

I'm sure my whole life flashed through his mind at that moment. When I was born, the day I nearly died, all the times he'd picked me up and held me in his arms.

All he wanted to do was love me and protect me, and he was looking at a nightmare, and it was killing him.

Actually, he was so angry I thought he was going to kill me.

My own son has made me mad a few times, but on the whole, he's been a much better child than me, I think. I will always remember that moment with my dad. All the anger and expectations and fear and love and pain and pride and disappointment and sacrifice were visible in his eyes.

That is the essence of what being a parent is all about.

Looking into the face of your kid who has no clue how much you love them and what you would do for them, and you know they won't really know until they have their own kid, and boy oh boy do you want them to know now!

Later on would be the trip to Appalachia, so his torment was really just beginning. What made it worse was that he had not been aware of all the trouble I was getting into until then. I got a lot of chances before they finally suspended me, so he really got an earful in the principal's office. Quite shocking, to say the least.

I was suspended a lot of times in high school. For smoking, for fighting, for cutting classes, you name it and I got suspended for it. I guess it doesn't really sound all that serious nowadays, it's not like I was a serial killer or anything, but I was definitely on the wrong track. The guidance counselors were tearing their hair out over me because they could tell I was pretty smart.

My parents knew that, too, of course, which was why they were concerned. I was grounded after that suspension, which I didn't take very well, and shortly thereafter I convinced my friend Laura that we should hitchhike to see her erstwhile boyfriend, Mike.

The rest, as they say, is history.

I think the incident in Appalachia scared my parents (it scared me, too!) and the session with the psychiatrist ended up being pretty helpful. I had been bored with school for some time and even told my father when he had to take off work to come to the school, but hearing it from the therapist seemed to finally get through to my parents. They put me in a work-study program at school so I could get out early every day as long as I had a job to go to.

I guess it's kind of ironic that, by failing to apply myself in school, something I was repeatedly warned would keep me from getting a good job and "succeeding" in life, I started my long working life and all the habits that would make me a success in my own right. I didn't want to go to school for the last half of the day, so I was pretty determined to work hard and keep my job.

Funny how things work sometimes.

I started off on the sheet machine at Busy Bee Dry Cleaners, "A Honey of a Cleaner," followed by a dental office and eventually a short order cook at a bar, although that was a night job.

I was passing my classes, but my home life was getting a little stressful. Even though I was working hard and keeping my grades up, I was still out getting high or drunk and coming home late, and that led to a lot of fighting with my parents, in particular my mother.

Now I understand she just wanted to keep me safe, but I figured if I was working and earning money, I was an adult and didn't have to listen to my parents anymore. Typical teenage stuff, trying to grow up too fast, not wanting to listen to anyone.

Eventually there was just too much conflict at home, and I moved out of the house and rented a room at a boarding house in Long Beach, on Long Island. I paid twenty-five dollars a week and had to take a bus to go to school, but if I hadn't have gotten out of the house, I swear my mother and I would have killed each other. On top of everything else, I was at that age when a girl is always arguing with her mother, anyway.

But I still wasn't satisfied. Now I wanted to get out of school for good, not just at noon, so I convinced them to let me take all my final exams early, and they did!

To be honest, I think they were probably as anxious to get me out of there as I was to leave. I did okay on the exams, got my diploma, and got the heck out of Dodge.

I had already decided I wasn't going to college; it just wasn't for me, so why on earth would I want to stay in high school any longer than I had to?

Once I was working the bar jobs, I didn't really want to do anything else because there was so much more money to be made than at a dry cleaners or a dental office.

There were also a lot of drugs. It was the late 70's, and pretty soon I graduated to cocaine from my previous pot smoking and drinking, which wasn't a good thing at all. But back then it was everywhere. You were considered strange if you didn't do coke. It was a dangerous time. People I knew would overdose in the bars, friends would deal drugs and get arrested, and while that never happened to me, I was always right on the brink. I was just too close to a lot of people who were getting in a lot of trouble.

After a couple of years of that nonsense, my father stepped in, and like always, did what he had to do. He and my mother had finally had enough of my bullshit, and so my dad shipped me off to where the real bullshit was located.

I was heading to Texas.

4

Lone Star

OF COURSE, MY FATHER DIDN'T JUST COME
by my little room and hand me a ticket to Texas, which
by the way is not where all the bullshit is actually located, at least not the figurative variety. You can find that
anywhere you go because it comes from individuals, and I certainly
don't want to disparage the Lone Star State in any way.

After all, Texas is where my son was born, so I will always have a
soft spot in my heart for the people and the wide-open places of that
great state, which was also where I really began my official, honest-
to-God adult life.

I was definitely not on Long Island anymore.

My father came to see me one day at the rooming house, which
I could tell was a painful thing for him to see because it was no great
shakes, this place.

What can I say? The place I lived in did not make him a proud papa.
It looked more like some derelict hotel than a place he wanted his
daughter to live, his little princess. I imagine looking at my room had
the same effect as that day he came to get me after I'd been suspended.

It was not what he wanted for me.

He sat down on my bed and gave me a very serious talking-to.

"Listen, I know you're on your own and you want to do things your own way, but this is no good. I met your boyfriend, I see your friends…"

He didn't have to continue. I knew exactly what he meant. I was running with the wrong crowd.

"You can't be a bartender forever. If you want to soar with the eagles, you can't hang with the turkeys."

That made me smile. It was one of those expressions I remember my father making all his own, like my mother and her "Take a long walk off a short pier!" all the time. I hear my parents say these things and actually thought they made them up until I got older.

My father was right, of course. I was seeing the same people on the same barstools every night, and some of them would probably be there in another ten years. Those that weren't were just as likely to be dead as wised up.

"You have to do more with your life, Carol."

That talk with my dad had a very big impact on me. My father had tremendous will power, and it was something I always admired in him. It was what allowed him to keep going every day, doing whatever he had to do to take care of us. My mother, on the other hand, possessed enormous inner strength, but was a little shaky on will power.

That was really the difference in a lot of their habits. My father loved drinking just as much as my mother did, for example, but when you're working three jobs there's just not time for it. Whereas my mother had time to drink, but she also had the inner strength to more or less handle the problems it caused, at least as much as anyone can.

They were each inspiring to me in their own ways. I wouldn't be the person I am today without the examples they set for me, both good and bad.

I had about $10,000 saved by that time, part of which came from the settlement from a car accident, and that was an awful lot of money in those days. So I gave it all to my dad to hold for me and took his advice, which was to go to Texas as a favor to another girl around my age whose parents were friends with mine.

Ann and I went to school together, but she was a good girl who had done all the right things. She lived a block over from us and was very quiet and studious. Ann went to college right after graduation just as every parent hoped their child would do, and had never been suspended or even gotten a reprimand from teacher in her life.

Basically, my polar opposite.

My father and her father had been talking, and they figured that since Annie was having a hard time coming out of her shell and I had pretty much broken mine into a thousand pieces, that maybe we could help each other. Annie would calm me down a little, and I would help her be a little more sociable.

Of course what eventually happened was that I corrupted her, but it seemed like a good idea at the time.

I got on a bus headed for Texas, which was an experience in itself, and met Ann down in San Antonio where she was living with her sister, who I could tell didn't really want her there. She lived with her husband and Ann hadn't found work yet, so it was uncomfortable all the way around.

Jobs were very hard to find in that area at that time, at least jobs for which Ann was both qualified and pleased with, and so we decided to go down to Houston to see if we could find something there. She had a geology degree, so her brother-in-law thought Houston, with all the oil and gas companies, would be a good bet. I was game because I knew I could always work as a bartender no matter where I went.

Her sister's husband loaded us both in the car and drove us to the Houston and left us there, two twenty-two year olds who knew nothing about the area, and we got a motel room and started checking the newspapers.

Of course, the first place I wanted to visit was a bar, so I dragged Annie out into the night as soon as the first sun had set. My job was to bring her out of her shell, right? Plus, you could meet a lot of interesting people in bars. Maybe even somebody with a job to fill or a place to stay.

Sure enough, we met Ailene.

Ailene was a very gregarious, friendly middle-aged woman who took a liking to us immediately, and when she heard we were looking for a place to stay, he eyes lit up like a slot machine paying off in silver dollars.

"You can stay with me!" She said. "I live in a big townhouse with plenty of room."

She said it was just her and three kids there because her bum of a husband was never around, and if we wanted to we could move in the very next day, no problem at all.

There would be, of course, lots of problems.

But we didn't know any better. We figured we had just lucked into meeting a nice lady at a bar with an empty house and had immediately solved one of our biggest problems, and so we agreed on the spot.

Twenty-four hours later we were standing at a corner ramp to I-10 with all our belongings on a blustery March day that quickly turned into night with no Ailene in sight. A woman we didn't even know dropped us off with our stuff, so it wasn't like we had someone to call besides Ailene, who wasn't answering her phone, or anywhere else to go, so we just waited.

This was in 1977, long before cell phones, so once an hour or so I'd trek to a pay phone down the street, but there was no answer. As I remember the two of us standing there next to the freeway like a couple of homeless people, which we pretty much were, I can't help but think of all the people you see nowadays at similar intersections asking for money, real homeless people in much worse condition that we were back then.

I really have to count my blessings every day to realize how far I've come.

Back to the two very naïve young women standing on the corner. Finally, Ailene answered the phone. She said she'd gotten delayed but would get there soon, but we ended up standing out there like that for hours, watching every car that drove past, not even knowing what kind of car she actually drove.

Finally, Ailene arrived, smelling of alcohol but just as friendly as ever, five hours late. She'd stopped at a bar on the way from work and it had been happy hour, so…

What had we gotten ourselves into?

After she told us that, we clammed up and rode the rest of the way to her house in silence. We were just happy she'd actually shown up, by that point.

When we got to her house, we were in for an even bigger surprise.

The place was entirely empty!

There was no furniture in the place, just blankets to sleep on and some boxes that served as a table so you wouldn't have to eat off the floor. It wasn't quite as bad as the frisky lesbian in Kentucky with the toilet in her kitchen, but it was close.

She was right about one thing, though. Her husband was kind of a bum. He was also there, which was the third surprise of the night.

I guess it served us right for moving in with a drunk we'd just met at a seedy bar called the Poop Deck.

We slept that first night huddled together on the floor under an old raincoat, but we were both so exhausted we didn't care. We made pillows out of our clothes and did the best we could. The place was nice, it was just empty, which made it a little scary. Like sleeping in a big empty tomb, or something.

I remember Ann being very upset and crying, so I consoled her the best I could.

Ailene worked at a decent job, but her husband was out of work. I really felt sorry for her kids, who were all grade school age. Especially the eldest, a sweet young girl named Penny who was just old enough to be mortified by how they were living. Apparently the family had just moved from Mississippi and were waiting on their furniture to arrive, but it never did, at least not while we were there.

They didn't even have a refrigerator, so we all lived out of coolers. Ann and I would bring home finger food from happy hour just to feed the children, which was terrible and depressing.

I was in better shape than Ann, though, because I could walk to the main road where all the restaurants were and get a waitress or bartending job, which I did very quickly. But Ann had a terrible time trying to find a job. She was a geologist, for one thing, but we also had no car, so you can imagine what that's like in a city like Houston, which is really spread out and had terrible mass transit compared to back east. The house phone was also turned off a couple of days after we arrived, which made things harder.

Penny confided in us that her father was an alcoholic and her mother had been lying about the furniture. Both her parents were alcoholics, really, but at least Ailene was functional. Her husband didn't even work, and was gone half the time. I think we were the first people Penny trusted that she could talk to, and since we were only about ten years older, she saw us as friends. For all I knew, we were her only friends. I felt really badly for her.

Our first day there we got a ride to a department store and we each bought ourselves a pillow, a blanket, a towel, and a wash cloth, and I lied my way into a job at a French restaurant called Ari's Grenouille, which I actually thought was Italian at first, if you can believe it. It was on the main road near the townhouse, and I assured the person interviewing me that I knew all about fine dining.

I thought serving food was serving food, but that was not at all the case there, as anybody knows who's ever been to a four star French restaurant can tell you.

Ann, who was the one who told me it wasn't an Italian restaurant when I told her the news, also tried to warn me about that.

"Don't worry, I can handle it," I said.

Not exactly.

It was the snails that gave me away.

I didn't even know what escargot was, and I certainly didn't know the proper way to serve them, so as soon as I just scraped them onto a diner's plate to the horror of the waiter I was assisting, the jig was up.

Why, I don't know, but even after the screwed up snails, my waiter still let me serve the dessert, which had to be flambéed.

Which was a real disaster.

I had watched him do it for another table, so I figured it was easy. Just light the thing, right? Wrong. Very, very wrong.

I took the special lighter and poured the brandy on top of the crepe, instead of around the crepe, which is the difference between flambé and charcoal, basically. Plus, I poured way too much of it, and instead of lighting the fumes at the edge of the pan, I stuck that baby right in the alcohol and the whole thing blew up right in the man's face!

Sure, I know all about fine dining, I'd said in the job interview.

Yeah, right.

It turned out the guy I nearly barbecued was a very prominent and well-heeled diner, very big in Houston real estate and one of their best customers. A real tycoon.

"What the hell are you doing?" He bellowed, and leapt up from the table like a scalded cat, which he very nearly was. The waiter was beside himself, the other patrons were screaming, and Ari Varoutsos himself rushed out of the kitchen, shoved me aside, and worked like a mad man to calm things down.

It was pretty chaotic, actually. The entire restaurant was in an uproar because of little old me.

Ari picked up the check for the table, which must have been astronomical because they were drinking some very expensive champagne, and when all was said and done, came back into the kitchen where I was waiting, petrified, to let me have it.

Only he didn't, not really. He was mad all right, and he yelled at me something terrible, but much to my amazement, Ari didn't fire me. I remember his face was really red and his veins were really blue, and just when he was really screaming, two of the other girls who worked there rushed in and screamed, "Don't hurt her!"

Don't hurt me? Was that even a consideration?

That startled me so much I burst into tears, and I guess Ari, who was actually Greek and not French, not that it mattered to me since I barely knew the difference, took pity on me. He calmed down quite a bit and shook his head like I was this pitiful thing he'd found by the side of the road.

"You don't know what you're doing, do you?" He asked quietly.

For some reason, the fact he was trying to be nice to me made me cry even harder, and I told him my story. Everything came out. My father shipping me to Texas, Annie and her job search, crazy Ailene with the empty house and bum husband and embarrassed daughter, sleeping on the floor, the whole nine yards.

"If I lose this job I won't eat tonight," I added, which was true. I was really counting on that meal break.

I even blubbered out something about being five hours late, which I don't think he even understood, but for whatever reason, he let me stay.

I never served again, but he kept me on.

Ari could see I was desperate, and that was probably what did it.

There's something about pure desperation that moves people. Either that, or he just couldn't take another second of raw, naked truth that was pouring out of me.

Once I had calmed down, he fed me and told me to come back the next day.

It was a quite a first day on the job.

I learned how to make sauces and set the tables, which are actually good skills to have, and worked there for another couple of months before I gave poor Ari a break and moved on to another job.

Even though my days of barely getting by are long past, I still remember the kindness of the man who took pity on a poor girl who just wanted a decent meal, and I try and help people like that if I can. You never forget your roots, or at least you shouldn't.

It was a crazy time, but at least I ate well.

5

On the Road Again

HOUSTON IN THE EARLY 80'S WAS A REAL boomtown. It was always pretty wild, of course. I mean, it was Texas, after all, and Houston was right on the gulf, filled with roughnecks and oil riggers and lots and lots of money. But at this particular time in history, it was especially crazy. The movie Urban Cowboy had just come out, and everywhere you went, there were guys who thought they were John Travolta and girls who wanted to be Debra Winger.

Okay, so maybe I identified a little with Debra Winger, too.

Also, the 80's were pretty notorious for cocaine, which was pouring into Florida and spreading across the country like a Texas tornado.

I was no stranger to coke, of course. I'd done my share back in my nightclub days in New York. As far as I was concerned, these Texans might know cows and oil, but there wasn't anything about drugs they could teach me.

You might say I went from Saturday Night Fever to Urban Cowboy without missing a beat.

But I was really hoping to do better, and after my rough start at Ari's, I finally caught a break and got hired at a bar called the Switchlight. It was Ari who helped me out, introducing me to the owner one night when he came in for dinner at the restaurant.

I don't know whether Ari was still being nice or he really wanted to get rid of me, probably a little of both, but he was a smart guy and obviously I was more of a bar girl than a fancy waitress.

Maybe it was my Long Island accent.

Anyway, he pulled me aside and introduced me to the owner of the Switchlight, a big guy wearing a cowboy hat and a thousand dollar suit, which wasn't at all an unusual combination in Ari's Grenouille.

"You sure you can bartend?" He asked, looking me up and down like he was appraising livestock.

Which he may have done in his spare time, for all I knew.

"Oh, yeah!" I said. "Piece a cake."

"Cause I heard about the crepes."

I'm sure all the blood ran out of my face at that point, because he busted out laughing and slapped his thigh hard enough to draw blood from lesser beings.

"That must a' been funny as hell!" He snorted, and I had to laugh, too. It was pretty funny, after the fact, at least. And I should have known Ari would have told him about it. Not just because it was a good story, but because they were friends and it might be of interest to potential employers if I nearly burned a customer to death at my previous position.

"His eyebrows will grow back," I said.

He just looked at me for a moment until he realized I was kidding, and then he laughed even harder. When he finally caught his breath, he offered me the job.

"You got spirit, kid!" He said. "But you sure you can handle a bar full of drunken roughnecks? They'll give you shit cause you're a girl, they'll give you shit cause you're pretty, and they'll give you shit cause you're a Yankee."

"Sounds like I'm getting shit no matter what," I said, and he laughed some more.

I hitchhiked to the bar the next day, which took me forever. There was no public transportation back then. I guess they figured everybody either had a car or a horse.

Ray, the manager, took pity on me and told me he'd make sure I had enough money to take a cab from that day forward.

The bar itself was just like the owner had described, a big old beer and a shot place, filled with oil riggers and cowboys who were eager to get drunk and give me a lot of crap.

And they did. They gave me grief every single night, but I took it because I needed the job and I needed the money. They were really no different and certainly no worse than the city guys in the bars back on Long Island. They wanted to get drunk and they wanted to get laid.

One of the problems was that, not only did I have a pretty thick accent, at least to the people in Texas – to me I sound normal! But I also talked really fast, which was quite a contrast because down there they talk really slow. So basically no one could understand a word I was saying. It was like I was from a foreign country, or something.

So it was really tough, but I was determined to stick it out. My parents didn't raise any quitters.

Then one night I stood my ground with the biggest, meanest roughneck in the place, and just like in prison where they tell you to challenge the baddest guy in the yard to earn your cred, as soon as I gave it right back to the guy, I was accepted into the club.

"Hey, Yankee!" He growled. "Cain't you understand English?"

I had just asked him to repeat his drink order. The bar was loud as hell and it was packed to the gills. I slammed down the bottle I was holding, walked around the other side of the bar, and looked him straight in the eye.

And then he stood up.

He was huge and I had to crane my neck, but I wasn't backing down.

"Yeah, I'm a Yankee," I said. "So what?"

"So why don'cha - "

"Look, Cowboy," I interrupted. "I don't care how much crap you give me, I'm not going anywhere!"

The guy just looked down at me like he didn't know whether to squash me or laugh at me.

"And if you wanna drink here, you better get used to it!"

He just kept staring down at me.

"So whaddya drinkin'?"

"Uh, Bud."

"Comin' right up!" I said, and went back behind the bar.

I guess a lot of the other regulars heard us, because after that I didn't have nearly as much trouble, at least from them. They still gave me shit, but it was more like they were giving shit to their kid sister. Kind of protective. They could pick on me, but nobody else could.

All told, I ended up having a lot of fun there. I met Red Adair, the big oil fire guy who was played by John Wayne in the movies, and a lot of other larger than life people. That's another way that Texas was like New York. Everybody's a character.

During this time, Ann got an office job across town, so we both moved out of the empty house and said a tearful goodbye to poor Penny and her crazy family. I really hope she got away as soon as she was able and bought herself some furniture.

Ann was working near the airport and found a little apartment near there, but that was way too far away from the bar, so I moved into a La Quinta Inn right off the highway for a few weeks until I made friends with another girl from the bar named Janet and moved in with her.

I even bought her car, which was a really nice Monte Carlo. I had the money for it pretty quickly because I was making all kinds of money at that place. The big drillers and the corporate oil guys all had tabs, and at the end of the month I'd get a percentage of the total, which was thousands of dollars. Plus, the guys who paid cash were liable to give me a twenty for one beer and let me keep the change, and that was when a beer was a dollar. It was crazy money. Ann had a good job with Fireman's Fund and I probably made more that she did.

So everything was going great. I was young, free, and getting rich slinging beer.

And then it happened. With me, something always happens.

One night a bunch of us from the bar were snorting coke after closing, and decided to drive out to the beach, stoned out of our eyeballs, for a barbeque.

Somehow I managed to step on a hot charcoal, which was incredibly painful, let me tell you.

My friends threw me in the ocean and then pulled the charcoal off, and a big chunk of my foot along with it.

"You'll be okay," one of them told me, before pouring Jack Daniels over my foot and wrapping it up in a beach towel.

The party continued.

Three days later I'm still in massive pain and trying to get by with aspirin or Tylenol or something, and Janet notices a dark line running up my leg.

"I think that's gangrene," she said.

Apparently I had a massive infection.

"Carol, you have to go to the hospital!"

But I didn't have insurance, so I went to the drug store pharmacy near the apartment. When I showed the pharmacist my leg, his jaw dropped.

"Honey, you need to get to a hospital right now. God only knows what kind of infection you have."

"But I don't have insur - "

"You could lose your foot," he said.

The thought of losing a limb finally got through my thick skull, and I let the pharmacist take me to the hospital. He just took me to the ER like it was a McDonald's drive thru and sped away. He didn't want anything to do with me, and I don't blame him. He was pretty nice to give me a ride, in the first place.

It was horrible. They had to cut out part of my foot, which was just as traumatic as it sounds, but at least I didn't lose my foot. I still have the scar, too.

For six months after that, I couldn't walk. I couldn't do anything, really.

So I did what any kid would do. I went home.

Defeated but not dead!

It was a little like my accident with the storm door. Suddenly I was back in my parents' house, being waited on hand and foot, especially foot. I was beside myself. I had finally gotten away from home and started to make a life for myself and there I was, back at square one.

I couldn't wait to get better and get out of there, and just as I was almost ready to leave again, my cousin Megan was having some trouble with a boyfriend who had taken advantage of her. She was only sixteen at the time, but like everyone in our families, she worked and made money, all of which she'd given to some boyfriend she thought she loved, who then broke up with her from Arizona. He'd gone there to set up an apartment for them, but after getting three thousand dollars from her, he sent her the Dear Jane letter.

She was devastated, almost to the point of a nervous breakdown, which really worried her parents. Megan was a good kid, not a rebel like me, but was really messed up over this boyfriend thing, and had started doing drugs. Her parents (my god parents) spoke with my father about it, and he decided to ask me to go with Megan to Arizona. She was going to go by herself come hell or high water, and he figured I could keep her out of trouble. My foot was getting better and my attitude was getting worse, so I figured, why not?

So instead of going straight back to Texas, I took a more circuitous route with Megan through Tucson so she could deal with this asshole boyfriend and get on with her life.

Three thousand dollars was a lot of money back then, but what she really needed was what everybody now calls closure. She needed to resolve for herself that this guy was a loser who had lied to her and didn't love her, so she could move on. Nobody expected he would have the money, anyway.

I knew him from the neighborhood; he was a no-good drug dealer. I thought she would be better off without him, but I was all for her confronting the guy to get it off her chest. Plus, she had a car, so it seemed like a road trip would work out for both of us.

Not exactly.

To start, it took us almost a month to drive to Arizona. Neither one of us knew how to read a map, and we started off going in the wrong direction and it was Delaware before we realized our mistake. Then we broke down in Tennessee in the middle of nowhere, just outside some little town where it took two days to get a battery for our car.

On top of that, some state trooper gave us a ticket for parking on the side of the road, and of course we had to pay the fine to him in cash. I paid him fifty-seven dollars in ones. The only motel was filthy, the only diner wasn't much better, and we were in a dry county so there was no booze within a hundred miles.

We found some derelict near the motel that charged us the outrageous price of seven dollars for a six-pack of beer, which we were happy to pay if it meant we could drown our sorrows for a night.

I called our dad who told us to just keep our heads down and get out of there, and if anything like that happened in Louisiana to keep driving, no matter what. He didn't want us to even stop to go to the bathroom in Louisiana, if we could help it.

We finally made it out of Tennessee, but we ran out of gas in Georgia. At night. In the middle of nowhere.

Actually, fumes took us to a little Texaco station, where we caught the proprietor as he was locking up. He was not a happy camper.

"I'm closed for the night!" He yelled.

"Please, please, we just need some gas," we begged, and finally he relented and let us buy his precious gas. He even let us use the bathroom! What a guy.

We further irritated him when Megan opened the trunk to get something, and then it wouldn't close. So now this poor guy is trying to fix the trunk, which he can't, so finally he just uses a coat hanger to hold it shut. We had to close it because everything we owned was in there.

So the guy has absolutely had it with us, by this time. Forty-five minutes after his shift had ended, and he was still messing with us.

Finally we head out, and after about ten minutes, my blood ran cold. I had left my purse, the one with all of our cash, in the bathroom at the gas station.

I screamed, Megan screamed, we both screamed all the way back to the station, where the guy was waiting with the purse.

I nearly fell to the ground with relief. I swear I wanted to kiss the guy, but he just held the purse out at arm's length and said, "Just go!"

He refused at first, but I made him take five dollars. After all that, he turned out to be a pretty nice guy.

We made it through Louisiana without anything terrible happening, and then Texas, and into Arizona before the next tragedy.

We made it to Tucson and stopped at a little place called Suds & Duds, which was a combination Laundromat and bar. We threw our clothes in the wash and went to look for some fun in the bar, which we most certainly found.

Too much fun.

By the time we thought to check the machines, somebody had

already emptied them. Now all we had was the clothes on our backs.

The dirty clothes.

I called my father and told him our clothes were stolen and we needed money, but I left out the part about getting drunk in the bar.

My dad, who was not a stupid man, smelled a rat and got the truth out of me pretty quick.

"Go to Goodwill," he said, and hung up.

So that's what we did. We bought cheap clothes at a second hand shop the next morning and set out for the other side of Tucson to find Johnny the bum.

He was not happy to see us.

We found him in a trailer park living with his mother. He had a broken leg, a broken arm, and a black eye. My first thought was that he looked like I thought he would look after we left.

Notwithstanding his injuries, I grabbed him by his shirt and got right up in his face.

"You owe my cousin three thousand dollars, asshole!"

"Get offa me!"

"Where's our money!" I screamed. Now it was our money. I figured after driving twenty-eight hundred miles, my cousin could share.

"I don't got it!" He screamed back. "Look at me!"

He did look pretty pitiful, I had to admit. Just then, his mother drove up and got out of the car. She could hear us yelling outside.

"What's going on here?" She demanded. "Who are these people? – Oh, hi Megan."

"Tell her, Megan," I said. "Tell her what her son did."

After Megan was finished with her tale of woe, Johnny's mother was yelling at him even louder, and hitting him as she screamed. "How could you do that to her?"

I almost felt bad for the guy. Johnny was getting it from all sides.

She kicked her son out of the trailer and told him to go find the money. As Johnny hobbled out of the trailer with his broken leg, his mother took Megan by the shoulders and said, "Never trust a man, honey. They'll steal every dime ya got."

When Johnny's new girlfriend showed up, she kicked her ass out, too.

We stayed in that sad, dusty trailer for a week until somehow, Johnny came up with some of the money he owed. Maybe a few hundred dollars, but it was enough that Megan felt vindicated, at least a little bit. I told her all the vindication she needed was to look around that trailer and thank her lucky stars she wasn't still with Johnny. I think it was a real wake-up call to see how she could have been living.

Johnny's mother was actually a very nice host, though. She drove us around and showed us the city, which was actually kind of ugly until you got outside of town and into the desert. She drank with us and smoked pot with us. She did what she could. I think she was pretty mortified her son had treated Megan that way.

As for Johnny, he hobbled out the door of the trailer every morning and returned that night with a little more cash to give to his mom to hold for us. She'd count it out, slap him upside the head, and make him sleep on the couch while Megan and I slept in his bed. God knows where the girlfriend was sleeping.

After a month on the road and a week in Hell, we were on our way to Texas.

6

Houston, We Have a Problem

W E FINALLY MADE IT BACK DOWN TO Houston, and now both me and my cousin were squeezed in with Janet in her little one bedroom apartment, which didn't go well at all. My cousin Megan was still a little freaked out about losing the love of her life to a trailer park hussy, and was a real bitch to our host. Before, when it had been just me, I had been cleaning the apartment and doing all that I could to make it worth her while to let me stay there, and of course I helped with the expenses, as well. But two's company and three's a crowd, as they say, and Janet and Megan just did not get along at all.

It got so bad Janet actually called my mother, who lent a very sympathetic ear.

"I know just how those girls are," she told Janet. "Why you let them in, I'll never know."

Thanks, Mom!

My mother was right, of course. One of us was tolerable, but two of us? No way. Especially since Megan was so out of sorts. I understood, though. It was really the first time she'd been out of the house.

First she'd had her heart broken long distance, then she left home for the first time on that crazy trip with me, then she'd confronted the moron who stole every dime she had, and now she was in a tiny apartment with someone she didn't know, in a place that was like a foreign country to her, and all before she could legally drink.

I guess I would be a little cranky, too.

At least she got a job really quickly so she had something to do. She started working for that same pharmacist who'd taken me to the hospital and saved my foot, typing those little labels for prescription bottles, and I went right back to the bar. We both got second jobs, too, because as I said, the kids from my old neighborhood worked. We both got out of Janet's hair as soon as we could.

Megan's second job was at a 50's bar called At the Hop, where she met and moved in with Lisa. I found a little studio apartment just before my father came down to check on the two of us. He'd been getting our periodic phone calls from the road and from Houston and finally decided he'd better come down.

He wasn't thrilled with the bar work and told me so. I think it was hard for him to imagine his little girl still serving drinks into middle age, which is probably where I was headed if something didn't change.

"Do something with your life," he told us both.

Naturally, Megan started selling coke on the side, because the Hop was a haven for high-end drugs at the time. Even I warned her about that one, and Lisa didn't appreciate it either because she didn't want that shit in her house. But Megan was making a tremendous amount of money and was very stubborn, so she didn't want to listen. And it wasn't like I was a saint in that area, either, since I was doing my share of coke and speed and pot, and the like. I just wasn't selling it from my job.

Speaking of which, my second job was horrible, but honest. A woman in the bar encouraged me to apply at a factory where she worked, which I thought was a crazy idea, but I actually passed a dexterity test and got hired by FMC Technologies as a shop helper, which basically meant I swept up and cleaned metal shavings from the machines and every other dirty, filthy job that my supervisor told me to do. FMC supplied equipment and technology for the oil and gas industry.

The woman who'd recommended me worked in another part of the building in a nice clean office, so I didn't see much of her after that, but I kept that job for two years, working seven to three five days a week and then going to the bar, which was where I met Cody.

Cody was big, handsome oil guy, but not a roughneck. He was a little higher up the food chain, which suited me just fine. He was a nice guy, kind of quiet, not a loud, braggart type like so many of the guys who came into the Switchlight. He was more cerebral, a thinker, and that really appealed to me. Maybe I was just ready to settle down after my recent misadventures, but whatever the reason, we clicked right off the bat. Meeting Cody changed my life.

Now when I say we clicked right away, what I mean was that as soon as he got off his barstool to ask me out, I liked him. But he took his time with it. He was a regular and I knew him as a customer, but for a long time I had no idea at all that he liked me.

As I said, he was a quiet guy. Some men would walk in the door like they were God's gift to bartenders and expect you to fall all over them, but Cody wasn't like that, and I think that was what attracted me to him when he finally decided to ask me out.

We started dating and right away he had a very positive impact on my life.

First, I got clean. Cody was very anti-drug, if you don't count alcohol as a drug, which nobody did in those days and most people still don't, and so I stopped with the coke and the amphetamines and all that nonsense. Cody was a responsible guy, the first man I ever dated, I suppose. He made the others seem like boys, by comparison.

Cody had been married before, was divorced but no kids, he owned his own house, and was basically just an adult with a real life and a real job. He was just what I needed at the time to straighten myself out.

I kept my day job, but Cody encouraged me to go back to school, which I wanted to do, anyway, so I cut my hours at the bar and enrolled at the University of Houston. I had always wanted to be a nurse.

Becoming a nurse turned out to be one of many things that didn't work out as I'd planned. But that's life. Life is what happens when you're making other plans, so you just have to make the best of whatever hand you're dealt and move on.

Things were going great. I had love in my life, I had purpose, and I had a cousin who was spiraling out of control.

Like I said, life happens.

I moved in with Cody after we'd been dating a while. He didn't pressure me at all, he just made the point in that analytical way he had that since he had this big house and was gone a lot on business, that I might as well take a vacation from paying rent.

"You deserve a break, Carol," he told me, and my heart melted.

Soon after that, we got engaged.

I really and truly believed Cody was the one. He snuck up on me a little bit, but when I fell, I fell hard. He swept me off my feet just like Richard Gere in An Officer and a Gentleman, only I kept working in the factory, so maybe that's not the best example.

But I was happy and I was in love, and that was all that mattered.

Megan, on the other hand, wasn't doing nearly so well. She continued with the drugs and the dealing, getting in further than even I realized. She obviously knew I disapproved, so she got very secretive with me, but I had my spies who told me what she was up to. Even Houston is a small town when it comes to the bar business, so I was able to keep tabs on her.

To be honest, I felt responsible. She was an adult and very stubborn, but I had brought her out here and she was, after all, my little cousin. It's like when you have kids. It doesn't matter how old they get, you always see them as children when they're in trouble, and I could see that Megan was heading for trouble.

My new life with Cody was wonderful, but it made me even more concerned about Megan. It seemed like the more responsible I got, the more reckless she became. I was worried one day I'd see her on the news as part of some drug bust or something.

Which was kind of what happened, actually.

But before all that, I finally found out what was wrong with me all those years when everyone just thought I was a klutz. The fall through the glass door, the uncountable cuts and bruises, the things everyone, myself included, had always just assumed were due to my excessive clumsiness, may have had a more sinister cause.

I had moved up a little at the factory and was now assembling butterfly valves, which meant better pay, but was just as dirty, if not more, than my previous job. The whole factory floor was just a grimy place to work, to be honest. When I went home at night, whatever they'd been painting that day in the shop would come out of my nose. It was all lead-based paint, too. Nobody knew the risks and nobody cared, either. It was a different time.

One day while I was at work, I came down with what I thought was a pretty hellacious flu, and it got so bad I had to leave my job and go to the doctor, who told me the same thing. I had the flu and should drink plenty of fluids and go home and take it easy, which I did.

Two days later I couldn't get out of bed.

It started with my feet, which suddenly became numb, like they were asleep. Only permanent, which is a very scary feeling. Everybody knows what it's like when your foot falls asleep, but what do you do when it doesn't wake up?

Naturally I couldn't walk, so Cody had to carry me to the car and take me back to the doctor, who by then knew enough to put me right into the hospital. I stayed in there for about a month while the doctors ran every test under the sun to try and figure out what was wrong with me. It was awful. When somebody came in who had suddenly lost the use of their legs for no apparent reason, they just poked and prodded until they ruled things out.

The first thing I endured was a myelogram, which is like a combination x-ray and spinal tap. Nowadays they would have done an MRI, but back then, it was a myelogram, which showed inflammation.

They gave me Decadron for twenty days straight, which is an old anti-inflammatory drug used today in chemotherapy. Today I don't think they give it to you more than six days in a row because it eats your stomach lining. It's very powerful stuff, and finally it did the trick and I was able to walk, so they sent me home. But they never really diagnosed me. I was told it might have been either toxic shock syndrome, an advanced form of syphilis, or multiple sclerosis, all of which sounded very scary to me.

Toxic shock syndrome, a potentially fatal bacterial disease, had been in the news recently because there was an outbreak linked to a new brand of tampons. Multiple sclerosis was not something I knew much about except that there was no cure, so I have to tell you I was praying for syphilis. At least I knew something about it and it was curable.

I was lucky that Cody wasn't offshore, so he was able to be around and take care of me, which he did in more ways than one. He told me everything was going to be all right, and that we'd get through it, which, true or not, was something I really needed to hear.

Especially since, on top of everything else, I was right in the middle of planning our wedding, which was only a few months away, set for the following April.

So I had a lot going on. And stress, as I would soon learn, was very bad for whatever it was I had.

At first it seemed like Cody had been right. Everything really was fine. I felt like I was back to normal, so I went back to work, Cody went back to work, and I didn't even have to see the doctor. Things were good.

Until the day I went blind at the mall.

I don't know if you've ever suddenly lost your sight, but for me it was even scarier than waking up without being able to move my legs.

Because I was walking at the time.

I was moving right along, enjoying all the Christmas decorations, weaving through the crowds of holiday shoppers, and suddenly all of that left me. There was only darkness.

I walked right into some store's plate glass window, which did not break, thank God, and hit my head so hard I knocked myself out.

The store was Texas State Optical.

Somebody up there was definitely watching over me, because at the moment I lost my sight, I literally walked right into the optometrist's.

The next thing I knew I was flying through the air, but it was really Dr. Lipsky carrying me into his store. I heard a very kind voice ask me what happened.

"I don't know, suddenly I couldn't see!"

He laughed. "You've come to the right place."

He examined me, called his assistant to examine me, then his daughter, who was another optometrist, to examine me, and finally he asked me if I'd been in the hospital recently.

"Yes!" I said. "How did you know?"

"Tell me what happened," he said, and so I did, the whole story, including the syphilis.

After I finished, he told me there was something very wrong, and that I needed to go back to my neurologist. "The problem is not with your eyes," he said.

It was really scary to hear him say that, but I will never forget how kind he was. Cody was offshore and hard to reach, but he couldn't have picked me up even if I'd gotten hold of him. This was all in the days before cell phones. And who knew what Megan was doing, but even if she wasn't getting into trouble she would have been at work, so there was no one to call, really. So Dr. Lipsky got in my car and drove me home, with his daughter following. Such a sweet thing to do.

I called my doctor the next morning and he told me to call an ambulance, which took me right back to the hospital. I still had not spoken to any friends or family or Cody. They ran some more blood tests, and finally the neurologist came in and gave me the news.

"You have multiple sclerosis," he said. Okay, so at least now I knew. But his next words really blew me away.

"There's no cure, and there's nothing we can do for you."

I'm sure he wasn't actually quite as cold as the quote from my memory, but that's exactly how it sounded to me. All I heard was "no cure" and "nothing we can do."

How many times has a doctor said that to you? I pray to God the answer is none, because it was just about the worst thing I could imagine hearing.

But I pressed him. I needed to know some things. Looking back on that day, I'm just amazed at how prehistoric it all seems.

"What happens now?" I asked.

"It's not good," he answered. "Basically, your life as you know it is over. You shouldn't work, you shouldn't tax yourself, you should just take it easy."

Take it easy? I wanted to smack the guy!

"You shouldn't have children, you shouldn't exercise…"

His voice droned on and on with all the things I shouldn't do. There was nothing that I should do. It was a very depressing thought, and one that I know has overwhelmed a lot of people with the diagnosis, especially back then when so little was known about treatment and therapy.

"Your life as you know it is over."

I couldn't get those words out of my head.

Finally I was able to get word to Cody, and then I called my parents, who were just as confused and scared as I was. Nobody knew what MS was back then, including most doctors. It was just something that happened when you were making other plans.

Like life.

I went back on anti-inflammatories and eventually I could see again, but it was a scary feeling. Suddenly I was worried about everything I did. I didn't want to drive because what if I went blind or my foot couldn't work the brake? There were suddenly so many other things most people take for granted that I now had to plan carefully.

I began to see what the doctor meant when he said my life as I knew it was over. Everything I did was affected by the disease or the fear of the disease from that day forward, and that has remained true, to a certain extent, ever since.

But there were two sides to that coin. There was the disease, and there was the fear of the disease. Maybe there wasn't a cure for MS, but there was a remedy for the fear. I didn't have to be afraid, right? Right?

To be honest, I wasn't sure. But I was going to try.

I'd always been a fighter, and I was in for the fight of my life.

7

Marriage, Mystery, and MS

NOBODY REALLY KNEW MUCH ABOUT MS back in 1984. My parents didn't even know what it was before they got the call that I had it.

Imagine getting a phone call that your kid has an incurable disease that you've never even heard of before!

So as devastating as it was for me, I can only imagine how my parents felt. When my son is sick, it hurts me so much as a mother, you can't believe. Especially given what I've gone through with illnesses, there is nothing I wouldn't give to take his place when he's sick or in pain. And he's gone through some of his own problems, believe me, which I'll get to later.

After the diagnosis I went through all the stages of grief and denial, like anyone would, but what really helped me through it all was Cody. He was my rock. He never wavered at all in his love and support.

A lot of things go though your mind at a time like that, as you might imagine, and having someone who loves you without exception can literally be a lifesaver. I'm sure there are many people whose relationships cannot survive something like that, so I give him a lot of credit for sticking by me during this time.

Especially when my darling cousin Megan moved in with us a month before the wedding and then promptly got arrested for selling coke at a fancy hotel, making all the local newscasts.

But I'm getting ahead of myself.

After the diagnosis I went back to work because I refused to let MS rule my life. Cody and I shared many hours together talking about things, but there was never any doubt we were going to move forward with our plans for a full life together. We were in love and we were together and that was all there was to it.

As soon as I was able, I went back to work and back to planning for my wedding the following April. Christmas was a little tough, but we got through it.

My cousin Megan, in the meantime, was not doing too well. She had really given in to the drugs and was completely out of control. As I said, I felt very responsible for her since I had brought her out her with me, and because we had basically grown up together. Her parents were my godparents and vice-versa, and she was like a sister to me.

So I asked Cody if we could take her in.

Looking back on it, I have to laugh at how audacious I was. We were about to get married, I had recently been diagnosed with an incurable, life changing disease, and oh by the way honey, can my drug addicted cousin come stay with us for a while?

Cody said okay.

There was discussion, of course. He was obviously not thrilled with the situation. But his heart was in the right place and he loved me, and ultimately we both figured it would be good for her to be in a stable environment.

Boy, were we wrong.

I shouldn't say wrong, I suppose. Of course a stable home is good for anyone. What we were naïve about was thinking a nice home in a nice neighborhood would automatically solve her problems. Drug addiction doesn't work like that. It's tough. I have since worked with a lot of addicts in my volunteer work, and sometimes it takes a very long time for a person to change regardless of how much help they receive. Some people don't make it at all.

But things seemed okay at first. I was working, Cody went back to work off shore, and Megan moved into the house with us. I thought maybe she could even help prepare for the wedding.

On that point, I was really wrong.

The luxurious JW Marriott Hotel had just recently opened up next to the Galleria shopping mall in a tony section of Houston, and apparently they didn't take kindly to drug dealers delivering cocaine in the lobby of their establishment, which was what Megan was caught doing about two weeks after she moved in with us.

Of course it was part of a sting and all caught on video.

So my mother and I, instead of shopping for wedding incidentals, we went shopping for a bail bondsmen.

Cody was off shore, which was probably a good thing because he might have killed her. He had been very understanding thus far, but harboring Pabla Escobar was probably a little more than he was willing to take.

I had no idea how the criminal justice system worked at that level, but by the time I got things figured out it was clear to me that I would have to use the money Cody had left for our wedding to bail my cousin out of jail. Apparently bail bondmen need collateral. Who knew?

I was beside myself. I didn't want to tell Cody, but I knew I had to. I didn't want to use the money for that, but I couldn't leave Megan in jail. It was an impossible situation. Plus, stress is not a good thing when you have MS, although that was another thing people really didn't know about the disease at the time.

Needless to say, I was furious. My whole wedding was now shrouded in the shadow of my cousin's drug bust. The police even came out to the house with a search warrant and ransacked the house; it was a total nightmare. And on top of all that, we found out later that Megan had been totally set up. She had been sleeping with the married cop who ended up arresting her!

I guess that was part of his fringe benefits or something. The more I found out, the more disgusted I was with the whole thing. The cop was thirty and she was eighteen, she'd been working at the hotel bar for a couple of weeks, and she was obviously singled out because she was young and naïve. Megan was asked to deliver a drink to one of the rooms upstairs, where a man would give her a package that she was then to deliver to someone else. It was very stupid on her part to trust these people, but it was very much entrapment on theirs.

This was a very international hotel, with lots of dignitaries and foreigners, particularly Mexico, and there were often secret service around because of the Bush family. So it was all a very big deal in the news for weeks.

But it was all bogus. They actually wanted someone else from At the Hop, someone Megan knew from her other job there. They figured they could scare her into testifying against him, but we looked into that possibility and it was clear she would have been killed. These same people later murdered someone we knew, forcing his motorcycle off the road. My cousin had been hanging out with some very dangerous people. People she knew nothing about, and the cops were totally willing to throw her under the bus to get at them. An eighteen year-old girl. Unbelievable.

We eventually proved entrapment in court and she got off with a fine and no more jail time other than the four days I was running around trying to get her out, with my apoplectic mother at my side, all after the cops had trashed our house. Cody was furious about that, of course. Nobody wants the cops in their house throwing things out of the closet and emptying drawers on the floor, none of which they put back. That alone was such a hassle, it's unbelievable.

They pounded on the door at eleven at night, marched in, and basically destroyed the place. My mother was drinking gin straight out of the bottle and I needed a couple of belts myself before calling Cody with the news.

It was miserable experience for us all, and if it hadn't been for the young defense attorney who basically fell in love with Megan who found out all of the seedy stuff with the cops, things could have gone very differently. A public defender might have backed her into some horrible plea bargain or something that could have ruined her life. After a number of years, she even got the felony conviction expunged from her record, but if it had happened today, she probably couldn't have gotten a decent job. Nobody did background checks back then.

But most of her legal dealings happened after the wedding, so at least she was out of jail until things got worked out. The wedding photos are a sight to see. My mother has no fingernails and Megan was still beat up looking from jail, which had not been kind to an upscale white girl with a New York accent. The pictures are a mess.

Really my worst moment was when I had to tell my almost husband that I'd spent our wedding money bailing out my cousin, which made him none too happy, let me tell you. Especially since she was in the wedding party. I can still see him looking at her out of the corner of his eye, holding in his anger for the sake of the ceremony.

He actually told me as soon as the wedding was over that Megan was not to be in our house and he didn't want me to ever see her again, which made me a little mad in spite of everything. She was still my cousin and I loved her like a sister, but I guess I could see where he was coming from.

At the time, Cody was up for a vice president's job at his company, which did a lot of business in Mexico. So even a whiff of connection to the drug business would have been a very bad thing for him. It was like someone had thrown a big rock in a pond and all the ripples were touching everything in ways we couldn't have imagined.

Megan and I didn't talk for a very long time after that, but eventually I got her a job at a local UHF television station and she parlayed that into bigger and better things and cleaned up her act in a big way. Within two years she was completely sober with a great job and has never done drugs again. To this day she goes nuts if that song Cocaine comes on the radio, she absolutely hates it. Megan is like one of those people who stopped smoking and then crusades against it. We're still very close and she's always been there for me when I've needed her over the years. Blood is definitely thicker than water.

But back to the wedding.

As I said, it was a little bit of a nightmare in the days leading up to the ceremony, but how can a girl not have a good time at her own wedding?

Let's see…my husband's family were all complete teetotalers, and my family drank like fish, so there's that, for a start.

Cody's family didn't even want alcohol at the wedding, but they gave in when I told them my relatives wouldn't come unless there was, which was not much of an exaggeration. They probably would have all brought their own.

"We can just serve punch and cake," his mother said to me. I pictured my own mother dropping her highball if she heard that. I put my foot down.

"My family expects booze, food, and more booze," I answered as sweetly as I could, and since the wedding was at our house and my husband was expecting sex on our honeymoon, we served alcohol.

You might think that his extended family would bond with mine over alcohol, but in this case, geography trumped the booze. The Texans and New Yorkers just didn't trust each other at all. It was almost like the second Civil War around the punchbowl.

I'm exaggerating, of course. It's not like fisticuffs broke out over the cake or anything, but it was a very strange experience to see grown men in huddles on each side of the room, eyeing each other like the Cowboys and the Giants. They really seemed like aliens to each other, I have to say.

Cody's family and mine could not have been more different, from upbringing to religion, but the one thing that had in common was good bourbon.

One thing that really impressed me about them, though, was that all eleven girls in his mother's family went to college. Cody's mother was the eldest, born right at the beginning of the depression on the family farm in tiny Winters, Texas, and yet she and all the others managed to get a higher education. I found that remarkable and still do.

They were all simple farm people at heart, even after they were educated. The best way to describe the difference from my family is that Cody's people are not fussy, whereas fighting and complaining is in my family's DNA. Cody's family didn't care about fancy things even when they had the money to buy them, whereas my family had no money but wanted all those things, anyway.

Cody had a younger brother and sister, Tim and Laura. After we were married, Tim was accepted into the Air Force Academy, and we had a party for him at our house. I made a big fancy dinner and set a beautiful table with our best china, napkin rings, and polished silverware.

None of Cody's family would take the napkins out of the rings. They thought it looked too pretty, and one of them even asked for a paper towel to wipe his mouth. I had to convince them it was okay to use the cloth napkins, which took some doing. When I served champagne, they all had a little sip. Very big deal. My family would have required a case of champagne and a keg of beer for backup.

Tim has spent his entire career in the service, and is now a lieutenant colonel, I believe.

Laura was a real granola type back then, the kind of Austin hippie who could go quite a while without shaving her legs or underarms, but she was also very smart. She's some kind of scientist now.

Cody, however, had not been particularly close to any of them for a long time before we met. He hadn't even spoken to his mother for three years when we started dating, something I found inconceivable. My family argued and fought all the time, but we were a family. Even now that we all have families of our own, I can't imagine letting years go by without talking to them.

I'd like to think his mother in particular appreciated the fact that I brought them back into their son's life. There was some bad blood with Cody's parents because he had divorced his first wife, which was a big sin to them, I think. They had also never helped him with anything like money for college. Basically he left home and that was the end of the support. They were tough, hardscrabble German farmers who didn't have much for a long time, and they just weren't loving people. They kept their emotions bottled up. Unless it was disapproval about divorce, I guess. That was okay to express.

Maybe if they'd opened a few bottles like my family, they'd have had a few more laughs.

An interesting side note to that was that Cody is the only one of his generation who had a child, our son Ryan. Both Tim and Laura had themselves fixed in their twenties, and even Cody did not want children at first.

I'm a firm believer that even people who think they don't want kids need only look in the eyes of their flesh and blood child to change their mind. I can't imagine life without my son.

Laura had been married young, but it didn't work out and was over early. She told me she had been abused by one of her uncles, and I think that really scarred her. The thing was, I was probably the only family member who believed her. She was a sweet girl who wouldn't hurt a fly, and there was no way in my mind that she would make that up.

Their whole family was odd in that way. Very distant. Family not talking to each other was a completely foreign concept to me. When I heard Cody hadn't seen his mother in so long, I made him take me to meet her.

"We have to go see your mother," I said.

"Why?" He answered.

"Because we're getting married, and you're her son, and that's all there is to it!"

So we went to see her. She met us on the porch, gave me a hug, and then shook her son's hand. "Hello, son," she said.

I will never forget that moment. She shook hands with her son.

My mother had always told me, and any mother will always tell her daughter, that you need to see your significant other around his mother. How a boy treats his mother tells you a lot about the man. At least I saw that Cody was very nice to his mom.

It was she who was very cold towards him.

Of course she would soften up considerably towards Ryan when he was born, because even a cold fish gets a warm heart for her grandchild.

But I realized why Cody was a little standoffish himself, a little bit colder than I was used to. It was because he was his mother's son.

She later confessed to me that she knew she had not been the best mother to Cody, and thanked me for allowing her the opportunity to spend time with Ryan.

"I did a much better job with him," she said, and she's right. She's been nothing but loving with my son.

If all of that earlier nonsense was just because Cody had been divorced, I have no idea. If it was, I think that's a terrible way to behave, and a lousy thing to carry around. I think Ryan helped her understand that.

But it's hard to know. No one can truly know what burden is carried by another person. If there's one thing I've learned dealing with MS, it's that you can't judge a book by its cover. You can't know the pain of another person, or really understand what they're going through, unless you've been there yourself.

We all just do the best we can with the hand we're dealt, and hopefully learn a few lessons along the way before it's too late to use them.

8

Highs and Lows

FTER ALL THE PROBLEMS LEADING UP TO the wedding, I was incredibly happy to get away from everything and go off to the Cayman Islands with my husband for a couple of weeks on our honeymoon, but even that had a few bumps along the way.

That's the story of my life, bumps along the way.

But mostly, it was a fabulous honeymoon.

It started off badly, though. We arrived at night and got on the shuttle bus that takes the arriving tourists from the airport to the hotels. We were both exhausted, but I was very excited as we drove past all these really terrific looking resorts, each one more fabulous than the next.

And then there was ours.

Our hotel was the last stop at two in the morning, everybody out, and it looked like a cross between that place my cousin and I stayed when we broke down on the way to Texas and the Bates Motel. It was almost scary looking, I'm not even kidding.

Maybe it was the lighting or the fact that it was so late, but as the bus was driving away I wanted to run after it and beg the driver to take us to one of the nicer hotels we'd passed on the way.

There was not really a lobby to speak of, just a room the size of a valet closet with a lot of keys hanging inside, but no one to hand them out. There was a pair of shoes in the center of the floor, and that was it. A half hour later the night manager sauntered up. I guess he was busy murdering some of the other guests. He took us to our room, put the key in the door, and the whole thing fell off the hinges, I swear to God.

At least we got another room.

During the honeymoon, I realized that Cody had lost a lot of trust in me. He thought I hadn't handled things very well with my cousin, and even though I did what I had to do, I could see his point. After all, I'd raided the joint bank account he'd set up for our wedding and subsequent life together without telling him first. I'm not sure what he expected me to do since he was offshore and hard to reach, but I got the general idea that maybe his first thought would have been to let her stay in jail, something I simply could not do.

Cody kept a lot of these feelings inside because it all happened so fast, and he was certainly not going to harp on it while we were on our honeymoon, but it was there just below the surface and we both knew it. Just how much was below his surface was something I would not find out until much later in our marriage. To me it was one of those bumps in the road that we'd get past and move on, but the trust issue was much bigger in his mind, I think.

But I wasn't paying too much attention to all of that at the time. I was just very happy to be married and on my honeymoon, and that was really all that mattered to me. I was in the Cayman Islands with my husband having a good time.

While we were there, however, Cody opened up some offshore accounts and transferred money there. It was his money and so it was in his name only, something that might have bothered me a little at the time, but it seemed mostly a reaction to the whole thing with my cousin, so I didn't worry about it. What I didn't find out until much later was that he would also end up transferring a lot of my money into those same accounts during our marriage, money I would never see again, money that effectively disappeared for all intents and purposes.

I can understand it to a point. His first wife had taken him to the cleaners, or so he said, and he was obviously trying to protect himself, especially after I used the money in our joint account for my cousin's bail. But he took things too far.

He would later purchase property through a shell company while we were married, again in his name only, something else he never discussed with me.

Don't get me wrong; I know Cody loved me. But it's almost like he began to hedge his bets as soon as the ceremony was over.

In retrospect, I don't know if he would have done all of that if it weren't for the incident with Megan and the bail money. Because of that, it was like a part of him decided I wasn't trustworthy, and so it became okay in his mind to deceive me.

All of this came out much later, of course, although there were clues.

I should have known from his relationship to his family that he had a dark side. He'd been perfectly willing to move on and never see them again until I insisted he do so, and that ability to move on without too much thought is something I can't understand. I've had friendships that I've had to end for various reasons, but family is different. There was definitely a colder side to the man I fell in love with that I never saw until much later.

But at the moment our door fell off, all I wanted to do was end our relationship with Norman Bates, who didn't seem all that shocked by what had just happened. He only laughed and left to get the key to another room.

I turned to Cody. "Is he kidding? I don't want another room. I don't want to stay here at all!"

"Carol, it's the middle of the night," he answered, "we'll find something else tomorrow."

Now I wanted to kill somebody. Forget Norman and his mother, I was ready to go psycho on someone, myself.

The second room was a disaster, too. It was so filthy I refused to even take my clothes off when I laid down on the bed. I don't think I even set foot in the bathroom. I just wanted to get some sleep and get the hell out of there in the morning, which we did. We complained about our accommodations and were given a beautiful condo that came with a catamaran and a scooter, and the rest of our honeymoon was wonderful.

Cody loved to dive, but because of a sinus infection I wasn't able to join him. However, I snorkeled and we did all kinds of other fun things that couples on their honeymoon did and generally had a fantastic time. The last thing on my mind was

After we came back home, it was back to work for both of us.

My MS was mostly at bay during this time, with just minor issues with fatigue and occasional numbness in my toes, but overall I was doing pretty well.

Still, I was not taking the diagnosis lying down, so to speak. If my doctor didn't know that much about the disease, I was determined to find someone who did. I researched everything that I could, and contacted the National Multiple Sclerosis Society, which referred me to a support group not long after my diagnosis.

I walked in, walked being the operative word, and was shocked at the atmosphere. Most of the others were in wheelchairs, and the overriding emotion was depression. Even the room was dark, which matched the mood of almost everyone there. Not that I blamed them; on the contrary, my heart went out to them. But I knew there had to be something more I could do besides waiting for the disease to overtake me.

There was no hope in that little room, and it would be ten years before I went to another MS support group. It was just too upsetting.

To be honest, I don't think my presence would have been helpful, either. I was walking and talking and working, basically still doing all of the things that most of them used to be able to do. I was a reminder of their former lives, lives they would never get back. And I was still grappling with understanding the disease. Over many years, I'm happy to say that I've learned enough to be helpful to others diagnosed with MS, but it took quite a while for me to get there.

Cody was very supportive of me. I told him I wasn't going to let the disease take over my life, and he encouraged me to take the bull by the horns and educate myself and look for ways to cope that had not been offered by my doctors.

"If you need to work less, that's okay," he told me, and that alone was unbelievably helpful to me, just to know that he would be there for me. He was really the one who first told me that I shouldn't wait around for the doctors, but to be proactive. Whatever happened between us later on, I have to give the father of my son the credit he deserves for sticking with me in sickness and in health.

I researched everything I could, which back then meant the library. This was all before the Internet.

Fortunately, Jacobs Engineering, which was where I was working, had a technical library with great resources, and a terrific librarian who helped me out quite a bit, finding people and organizations to contact. She helped me find out about a study for an MS drug, which was fantastic because back then there was nothing like that to treat MS. Sure, they used drugs to alleviate the symptoms, but there was nothing yet on the market specifically for MS. Everyone who was diagnosed was told the same things I had been told, which, in a nutshell, was "wait around to die."

Finding Dr. Rolak at the Baylor College of Medicine was a turning point for me. He was very positive. "If you want to exercise more, I think you should," he said, which was the opposite of what I'd been told before. Rolak had a lot of good ideas, and was very upbeat and open to new ideas. He was conducting a study on Copaxone, which was not yet approved for use for MS. I didn't qualify for the study because they needed people whose MS was currently active, but he was very encouraging. I felt a lot better after speaking with him and his team.

Between the time I left that first support group meeting and the time I met Dr. Rolak, I had been pretty depressed about the whole thing. I was drinking a lot and feeling sorry for myself, and he gave me reason to hope. Even though I couldn't get into his study, the fact that there was someone out there trying to do something about the disease was a blessing.

When I volunteer today, I remember what a difference Dr. Rolak's positive attitude made on my own, and I try to do the same for others.

I was eventually referred to Dr. Michael Newmark, a neurologist at Kelsey-Seybold, which is a great group of clinics in Houston that treat everyone from visiting Saudi Royalty to astronauts from NASA. He's still there, I think.

The waiting room was crazy, with all kinds of people from children to the elderly. I took a number and waited for what seemed like hours. Doctors and patients would come and go like it was Grand Central Station, walking out and calling names. At one point this shambling mess of a man came out who looked like Groucho Marx. He had the glasses and mustache and everything. I was just thinking that I hoped he wasn't my doctor when he looked down at his clipboard and called out my name.

Oh, boy.

"Right here," I said, and followed Groucho into the back.

Newmark turned out to be a little nuts, but he was also very positive, and he agreed to work with me. I got another lesson in books and their covers with him. "I don't know too much about MS, but I'm willing to learn along with you."

And he did. Like Dr. Rolak, he didn't tell me not to do things; he let me do what felt good and then analyzed how it affected me. He put out feelers on my behalf for other studies and treatments, talked to me about what was working and what wasn't, and even looked at Rolak's study to see if there was anything there that could help.

I hooked him up with Rolak's team and they began to communicate. After I'd go to see Rolak and ask questions about his study, I would tell Newmark, and we tried things. When I told him that Rolak was working with B-12 shots or cortisone to help with inflammation, Newmark would try it with me. It was like I was creating my own little study. Newmark was open to trying whatever I found out. I was pretty lucky to have found him.

Rolak couldn't tell me about all the experimental treatments, but whatever was out there in the mainstream and already approved for certain uses, he shared with me.

Valium was being prescribed to relieve stress, which everyone agreed was a major problem for people with MS, which was why the first doctor told me not to have children. The thinking was that having and raising a child was stressful, which of course it is. But now it's known that a lot of women with MS actually stabilize during their pregnancy, although a relapse after the birth of the child is quite possible.

As I see it, any young person out in the world working and having a life is going get stressed out over something.

So I got Newmark to prescribe Valium, which also helped with my leg spasms. But I was having lots of little attacks, which meant I was exhausted a lot of the time and would end up on my back in bed, unable to do a whole lot.

Then Cody lost his job.

In the early eighties, oil prices spiked after the energy crisis of the seventies, but a few years later there was a glut on the world market, and in 1986 the price dropped below ten dollars a barrel. A lot of the oil business was decimated, and Cody's company had to let him go. Houston was obviously hit pretty hard, so it was bad times for a lot of people down there.

Losing his job hit Cody really hard. That job was his identity, and being out of work was devastating for him. It was the whole 'breadwinner' thing, but magnified because he also had a wife who was sick a lot of the time.

He was out of work for six months, and the only thing that could have made it worse in his mind was if he also had children to support.

And then I got pregnant.

I was pretty shocked, being that I was on the pill and supposedly had hormone levels that made pregnancy unlikely. I was also on a steroid treatment that would not have been healthy for a baby.

"You're wrong," I said. "I can't get pregnant."

The doctor just shook his head and smiled. How many times had he heard that one?

"You're having a baby," he said, and closed my chart. "Any questions?"

I had plenty. Like how was I going to tell Cody? But that was something the doctor couldn't really help me with.

I made them do an ultrasound, and sure enough, there was a child growing inside me.

It was a little overwhelming, but deep down, I was happy. Deep down, I knew it was right. And deep down, I knew there would be trouble.

Cody had made it perfectly clear to me before we were married that he didn't want children, and I had agreed, although reluctantly. His brother and sister had actually had surgery in their twenties to prevent having children, as I've already explained, so I knew this was going to be tough for him to accept.

Not to mention the fact that he had been out of work and I had been told by my doctors not to conceive.

But most women, at their core, want to be mothers. Even the ones who don't think they do. I looked at the fuzzy image on the ultrasound and saw life, life that was created by God, life that would spring forth from my womb me and make me a mother. How could that possibly bring me anything but joy?

I thought of all those TV shows and commercials with happy young women breaking the news to their equally happy young husbands, where everyone laughed and hugged and told their partners how much they loved each other, and somehow I just couldn't quite see my news unfolding in exactly the same way.

At least I could give Cody my Valium.

9

And Baby Makes Two

ODY AND I WERE NOT IN BAD SHAPE FINAN-cially like a lot of people we knew during the oil bust of the eighties. Houston was really hurting and it seemed like everywhere you looked there was another foreclosure, but we had some money saved and didn't have a lot of debt like so many others we knew. Cody knew there were no jobs in the industry to be had for a while, so he went back to school to get a degree in electrical engineering and ride out the downturn. The oil business is and always has been boom and bust, but if you're smart and you plan, you can make it through.

Cody was smart, and he was always had a plan.

Having a child, however, was not part of that.

I have to stop here and tell you how much Cody loves our son Ryan, and has always been the best father he could be. Whatever problems we had in our marriage, neither of us would change anything about our son.

But before he was born, it was another story.

When I came home that night with the news, Cody was not happy. It was a very tense conversation, to say the least. He kept saying over and over how he couldn't understand how it had happened, and of course, all I could do was agree. I didn't understand it, either.

Finally he just went to bed. It was a lot to take in and I think he needed to retreat into his own head, get away from me, and not talk about. The next morning he told me he wanted to talk to my doctor, which I expected.

"This isn't good for you, Carol," he said, and I knew he was right. But that didn't change what I felt in my heart. Still, I understood we had to see the doctor. Of course we had to see the doctor.

And I knew what I was going to say to the doctor.

The same thing I said to Cody when he told me over coffee the next morning that I shouldn't have the baby.

"Cody, they told me I shouldn't exercise, and I've been exercising. They told me I shouldn't work, and I've been working. Everything they tell me not to do, I do, and I'm doing okay."

"This is different," he said. And I knew it was. But I also knew it was right. I had never been more certain of anything in my life. I wanted to keep my baby. It was probably going to be the only chance I'd ever have to be a mother, and there was no way I was giving that up.

So it became a big brouhaha.

All the doctors agreed with Cody that having a baby was a very bad idea because of my MS, and so there was a lot of pressure on me from everyone to have an abortion. It actually started to fracture my marriage.

I could see Cody's point of view. He was worried that he could lose me, or that I could end up so damaged that I would be in a wheelchair and he would be caring for both an invalid and a newborn. I hate the word invalid, by the way. There is nothing invalid about having a disability. But I understood.

Honestly, he was just very scared, and I certainly couldn't blame him for that. I was frightened, too. But I wanted the baby. To me, being a mother trumped everything. And this was my only shot. Plus, I had faith that the good Lord had not allowed me to get pregnant against all odds just so that I could get an abortion. I really had faith that things would work out.

So it made for a very stressful pregnancy, to say the least.

But my problems were all external. Ironically, I actually had a very smooth pregnancy, physically speaking. I never had an attack, never had any real problems. It's interesting because for many years, women with MS had been told not to get pregnant because it will cause flare ups of the disease, but later studies have shown the opposite, that being pregnant can actually reduce the number of attacks.

I find it miraculous that a disease that's worsened by stress can actually calm a woman's body when she's carrying a child. I'm pretty sure they have even developed a drug based on the chemicals or hormones released during pregnancy.

I even worked right up until I went into labor. Ryan was due on November 27th, and two weeks prior to that I took off work to see my doctor, and he told me I was in labor. I had been so busy at the office I hadn't even realized it!

He put me into the hospital and scheduled a cesarean for the following day.

My home life leading up to that point, however, was anything but smooth.

Cody was miserable the whole time, and not being very nice about it, either. And he only got worse as time went on. He left school with his degree and took a job way below his pay grade, which he hated. But we would need the money and possibly the health insurance, even though I was still working. We were still doing okay, but he went from the high six figures to about thirty thousand a year and that was just another thing that added to his general level of anger.

After Ryan was born, I had a major attack, which was expected, and I was off work and mostly housebound for about four months. Both my parents came to help me at different times, but Cody's parents, who I don't think had ever taken a vacation in their lives, decided to go to New Zealand after their first and only grandchild was born, which I thought was pretty strange. His mother was a nurse, too!

My mother traveled from New York and stayed for a month, but my mother-in-law, who only lived fifty miles away, never even so much as offered to babysit. Maybe she figured she would only make things worse with Cody given their relationship, but still. The first time she had Ryan for an extended period of time was after I divorced her son.

Fortunately, I had a lot of good friends who helped out, and of course every time I looked into Ryan's eyes, it was all worth it. He was the most adorable child I had ever seen. But it was a very, very tough time.

My mother was actually able to help us hire a nurse because she'd come into a small inheritance, so that was a real blessing.

To Cody's credit, he was very good with his son. They bonded immediately, and he was great about getting up and making the formula and changing diapers, none of which I could do for some time because of the attack. He was great with his child, but as much as I hoped that our beautiful son would bring us back together, it was not to be.

As sweet and loving as Cody was with our baby, he was sullen and distrustful of me. He had never wanted children, and since I had MS, I never thought I would have kids, either. And like so many problems in a marriage, it was a non-issue until it actually happened. After I got pregnant, everything changed. Cody had not signed up for a family. Neither had I, really, but life is unpredictable, and no one can ever know exactly what God has in store.

Even though there was never any questioning his love for Ryan, it seemed like Cody resented me from the moment I got pregnant, and he never really lost that feeling. He was fine when my mother was around, helpful and polite, but he was very cold to me, otherwise. There was simply no love or tenderness for me at all, and that was very depressing to me. I had this beautiful new baby and the man with whom he had been conceived wanted nothing at all to do with me.

It was devastating.

As a consequence of our discord, we both drank too much, which of course only made things worse. We argued constantly, and Cody started to get physical with me. And me with him. Things got very bad, and our marriage went downhill very quickly.

During that time I had pretty limited mobility, but I was not bedridden, and I was certainly no shrinking violet. Timid is not a word anyone would ever use to describe me. If Cody yelled at me, I gave it right back to him. If he pushed me, I shoved him right back.

Then Ryan got sick, and spent a couple of weeks in the hospital. I was with him in quarantine because they didn't know what was wrong with him at first. Cody couldn't even come into the room; he had to watch his son through a window. Ryan had a very high fever and lost half his birth weight because he kept vomiting, which was unbelievably scary. To see my tiny child with IVs and machines all around him was a horrible experience for us both.

They never found out what was wrong with him, but eventually Ryan got better and we got to bring him home. Since I'd been away from work so much, Jacobs Engineering let me go, but they gave me a very nice severance package and treated me pretty well, all things considered.

It actually worked out great for me because after that I went to work for Hyatt, and they loved me because I was able to bring in a lot of medical business because I knew so many doctors from all my MS research. Hyatt had never done too much medical business at that time, so I became their darling.

Doctors are always having meetings and seminars and conventions, and they spend a lot of money. As a result, Hyatt a lot of money, and they rewarded me in kind.

They even paid my salary while I worked on special projects for some of our clients' doctors, like the time I performed a travel feasibility study for the Baylor College of Medicine at the request of the world-renowned surgeon, Doctor Michael DeBakey.

Meeting him turned out to be pretty good for me, too.

DeBakey was an incredible cardiac surgeon, and people came to Houston from all over the world to see him. He was a dear and very helpful to me whenever I had a medical problem, but working for him was really difficult. Just imagine trying to make sense of a bunch of doctors' hand-written expense reports!

But while my career was going very well, my marriage was falling apart, and I finally decided to file for divorce. Cody was getting more and more comfortable settling our arguments physically, which I just couldn't tolerate anymore. Once he crossed that line, I knew it would only get worse, and I was not physically capable of defending myself.

And if things couldn't get more stressful, right in the middle of our nasty custody battle, I was diagnosed with thyroid cancer.

This is where my friendship with Doctor DeBakey made such a difference in my life. What he did next was truly amazing.

Doctor DeBakey found out about my diagnosis and immediately got me a suite at Methodist Hospital where he worked, checking me in and lining up some of the best doctors in the field to treat me, and I never once saw a bill. I wish everyone could have a friend like Doctor DeBakey.

I received more bad news when the doctors discovered that the cancer had spread from my thyroid to my larynx, so any surgery was extremely delicate. There was no guarantee that I would ever be able to speak again.

My dad came down to help me find a lawyer right away. Since Cody and I were still married, if there was an emergency of some kind and I was rushed in for surgery, he could legally make medical decisions for me that I wouldn't want, like allowing the doctors to just remove my voice box altogether.

Which I would not have put it past him back then, just to get me to shut up.

So it was a very scary time, but my dad was great. He stayed with me in the hospital, got me a lawyer right away who drew up a medical power of attorney so that Cody could not make any of the medical decisions, and absolutely refused to let anyone remove my voice box. They were operating right next to my carotid artery, so it would have been a lot easier for the surgical team to just take out the larynx to avoid complications.

Don't get me wrong, if it was a matter of life and death, I would have chosen to lose my voice, but over the years I'd grown pretty attached to it and I liked using it, so that had to be the last resort.

My surgery lasted seven hours and I couldn't talk for three days, and the whole time I was waiting on pins and needles until they figured out whether or not they would have to go back in and take my larynx. It was nerve wracking, to say the least.

My father helped me get through it. He was very cute, writing to me on a little blackboard just like I had to do, even though he could have just spoken to me.

There was nothing wrong with my ears!

We had a good laugh over that. He was right there with me all the way, just like he had always been. I was still his little princess.

Finally, we got word that they would not have to remove my larynx.

But my troubles were not over.

During this whole ordeal, Cody had been trying to get custody of Ryan because I had MS, and so as soon as I got out of the hospital I had to go right back into the legal fight. He was claiming I was an unfit mother because of my illness. Cody thought if I got custody, I'd go back to New York and take Ryan with me, and he was right. That's exactly what I would have done.

For legal reasons, I also had to move back into the house I'd shared with Cody or else my attorney thought he would claimed abandonment, so I went back there with Ryan not long after I got out of the hospital and moved into the spare bedroom.

Which was as terrible an idea as it sounds.

Ryan was about eighteen months old at the time, and one night after I'd finally gotten him to sleep, Cody and I got into another argument. He'd been drinking and was in a perfectly foul mood. To my horror, Ryan heard us arguing and came out of the bedroom, which was awful. I hated seeing his sleepy little face, confused and scared that his parents were fighting.

I scooped him up and ran back into the bedroom, locking the door behind me. I figured Cody would leave us alone and that would be the end of it, but I was sorely mistaken. No sooner had I turned around to put Ryan back in bed, than Cody kicked in the door and came towards me, wild-eyed and furious.

I was so shocked I literally had no time to react, and Cody ripped Ryan from my arms and threw him on the floor, something I will never, ever forget if I live to be a thousand.

Cody then proceeded to choke me. I had just gotten the stitches out after my throat surgery, so it was pretty intense. He knew that I wasn't even supposed to turn my head, let alone twist and abuse my neck like that. At that moment, I believed I was going to die, but even worse, I was going to die in front of my son, who was cowering beside the bed, and there was nothing I could do about it.

Just as I started to lose consciousness, I felt something heavy next to my hand below the windowsill where he had me pinned, and I managed to lift it like a club and hit Cody across the head.

It was a wooden airplane that my brother had sent Ryan from Germany for his first birthday, and it knocked Cody unconscious. I hit him again and then grabbed my screaming son and ran barefoot from the house into the cold February night.

I knocked on several doors before someone finally let me in, and called Martha, who was Ryan's babysitter and a wonderful friend. When she came to get me, I told her what happened, and all she said was, "Let's wait a bit before we call an ambulance."

At that point I really thought I had killed my husband, but he was taken to the hospital and survived with a hundred stitches and a hell of a headache. He never told anyone I had hit him because it had been self-defense, but that was effectively the end of our marriage.

Even after all that, he wanted to get back together, but there was no way I could do that. He claimed he had blacked out and didn't remember what he'd done, something I believed because he was an alcoholic. But that was still no excuse for any of it.

We went to see a counselor, and he gave her the same story, that he blacked out and didn't remember anything, but even the therapist wouldn't have any of it. He apologized profusely, but the fact remained that he could have killed Ryan, and he could have killed me. And I very nearly killed him with that damn airplane!

The counselor told us that someone was going to end up dead if we kept going like we were going, and that it had to stop. There was no saving our marriage.

It was a crazy ride, and it was finally over.

Even after he accepted that the divorce was going to happen, he didn't really seem to believe that it was over between us.

"I love you, Carol," he said, "and I'm going to make this all better."

But he was still drinking, so I knew that wasn't happening.

"You have your attorney, and I have mine," I told him.

"You'll come back to me," he said.

"Whatever."

So I stopped talking to him and let the lawyers handle it. I wanted to just take my son and go, but Cody was fighting that. He was fighting for his child.

But he was also all about the money, so I gave up the house and told my attorney I just wanted the car and my kid and that was all, and that's what I left the marriage with.

I also agreed not to leave the state of Texas for two years. Cody was smug about that, telling me that I would be "begging to come back," and maybe he even believed that, but two years to the day after my divorce was finalized, I was gone.

My attorney thought I was crazy to give Cody everything he wanted, but I just wanted out. "Forget the house and the furniture," I said. "Forget his 401K."

Truthfully, I would have given Cody my money to be done with him. I just wanted to take my son and end the madness.

I think the separation made him a better father, though. Once I had left the state of Texas and we were separated by thousands of miles, he realized what he'd lost. Cody worked hard all year without a break so he could spend the whole summer with Ryan, and they developed the close and loving relationship they have today.

Getting to that point was tough, however. I moved into a crummy little apartment without a washer and dryer and made do. It was better than living on the streets, but it was quite a difference from the home I'd given up. Visitations were tough because Ryan would sometimes cry and hold onto his daddy's leg, which broke my heart. I hated that he had to go through all of that, but all I could do was love him and try to get through it.

To his credit, Cody never missed a visitation, and always paid child support, although he could have afforded more. I wasn't going to challenge him on that, though, as long as everything else was peaceful.

We made an agreement that neither of us would ever bring anyone home when Ryan was around so that he wouldn't be confused, and we both kept that promise. I dated during that time, but Cody never did. To this day, he has never remarried.

At a particularly low point during that two year period, I called my mother and told her that maybe Cody had a point, that maybe I wasn't a good mother and I wouldn't be able to take care of Ryan and myself, but she snapped me right out it pretty quickly, in her typically direct way.

"You've been taking care of yourself your whole life, Carol," she said. "You can do this."

That was exactly what I needed to hear, and I realized she was right.

After that, whenever I felt sorry for myself or had doubts, I just thought back to my mother's words.

"You can do this."

Just like all the doctors who told me that I couldn't exercise, couldn't work, couldn't have a baby, couldn't do this or that or the other, I had always just gone and done what I wanted to do.

There was no point in changing, now.

10

Heading Home

MY TWO YEARS IN LIMBO WAITING TO leave Texas wasn't all bad. For the last several months I got to move out of my little apartment and live in a mansion, thanks to another very good friend, Howard Findlay.

I have been blessed with great friends over the years, and the secret to having good friends is to be a good friend, yourself. The Golden Rule really works, believe me.

But down in Texas, since Cody had lived there all his life and I was a relative newcomer, a lot of our friends didn't have much to do with me after the divorce since they had known Cody a lot longer, which is the way things happen after a couple splits up. People choose sides.

But there was one of Cody's friends I knew from my bar days who was different, and that was Howard.

When Howard found out where I was living, he would have none of it. He was a very wealthy guy with a lot of properties, and was planning to sell the house he had lived in with his wife before she died a couple of years prior, but he wasn't in any hurry.

He insisted I move in there with Ryan, who he loved and always called "Cowboy," and so suddenly I was living in a beautiful, furnished home with a live-in maid and gardener and I didn't have to pay a dime for any of it, not even the utilities.

Howard even took Ryan up to his ranch outside Austin and taught him how to ride a horse, and I worked for him on occasion, catering some of the big parties he held there. Howard was a really great friend at a time when I really needed one, and he made a big impression on Ryan, as well.

But my plan was still to move back east to be closer to family, so as soon as the two years were up, I gave Cody my thirty day notice and flew to Harrisburg, Pennsylvania, where a headhunter had gotten me an interview with Marriott to be their national sales director.

On the plane, I met a good-looking Italian guy named Joe, and we hit it off right away. He was from the east coast, which made me feel right at home. He worked for a big software company and often stayed at the Harrisburg Marriott where I was headed for my interview, and he kept tabs on me after that first meeting on the plane.

When I got the job, he found out about it about it and sent me yellow roses, which was nice. We ended up dating, so I got the guy and the job.

Lots of changes in my life, all happening at once.

The job was commensurate with my previous position and experience, but I hated it and I hated Harrisburg. There really weren't any national companies headquartered there, so since Harrisburg is the capital of Pennsylvania, I dealt with a lot of political people, state congressmen and the like, as well as a lot of trade associations.

The people I dealt with bored me. Nothing personal, I was just a different type of person than they were. I grew up in New York and then lived in Houston. Harrisburg was like a one-horse town by comparison. Nothing to do, nowhere to go.

It took me quite a while to even find a decent place to rent. I sure wasn't going to buy a house there, I can tell you that. I went up in the summer, so at least Ryan was with his dad while I looked for a place for us to live.

I stayed in the hotel while I looked, and then when I finally found an acceptable rental, I couldn't help but notice the three smokestacks across the street.

"What are those?" I asked the realtor.

"Oh, nothing," she answered. "Just Three Mile Island."

Great.

She told me that little nuclear meltdown had been such a long time ago, and everything was now perfectly safe, but still.

At least I got free electric with the lease!

So I got settled in time to get Ryan enrolled in kindergarten, and I actually did really well in the job, which was actually for the management company that Marriott contracted to take over and improve their under performing properties. Basically, our job was to analyze, streamline, and replace, and that's exactly what I did with the sales department. I'm very good at identifying problems and then figuring out how to solve them. A lot of it was just dealing with people, and I'm a people person. I can talk to anyone.

I did so well that they put me in charge of two additional properties, one in Maryland and one just outside Philadelphia.

I was kind of hoping they would transfer me, but instead I flew puddle jumpers every couple of months or so to keep tabs on everything.

But things were going reasonably well. Joe worked for a really big software company and flew all over the country, but he lived in upstate New York and we saw each other every other weekend, which was a nice way to get to know each other over time and still keep a little space. Ryan was still young, and I wasn't sure if I wanted to jump into another serious relationship right away, but Joe and Ryan got along really well and so I thought maybe Joe was a keeper.

I would soon be disabused of that notion, but for a while, it worked.

Meanwhile, I found a very good neurologist while I was in Pennsylvania who knew about a new drug coming out that had been approved for MS patients, part of the Interferon family. There wasn't very much of it, so it was only going to be available by state lottery, and he put my name on the list and got it for me because Pennsylvania didn't have a lot of people who applied, apparently. It was a very big deal to get it because I think the allocation was for only two thousand people, nationwide.

I remember my heart going out to a woman I saw on the Phil Donahue Show who was in very bad shape and had not gotten the drug, so I was extremely grateful my name had been selected.

My doctor didn't even specialize in MS, either. It was just another example of how God truly blessed me. In spite of all I've gone through, I have an awful lot to be thankful for, and I'm reminded of that every single day.

The drug was not easy to use, however. It was a powder that had to be mixed with a liquid, and then injected with a needle. I was told to practice on an orange first, and to call my doctor right away if there were any flu-like side effects like fever, headache, nausea, or vomiting.

And that was all the instruction I got.

The drug wasn't a cure or anything, but for some people it slows the progression of the disease, as it has for me.

I had been doing better after I left Texas because just getting away from my ex meant I had a lot less stress in my life, but I would still suffer the occasional attack and so was eager to try the drug.

It was rough in the beginning because nobody really knew all that much about the drug. I would take it in the morning before I went to work and then get horrible chills, but I was afraid to tell anyone because I didn't want them to take me off it. I asked my doctor for the names of other patients who had received the drug so I could compare notes, but he wasn't allowed to provide that kind of information.

Basically, I was flying blind.

I think there was some problem with the FDA, and as a result information just wasn't filtering down through the system, which can be a real problem in health care. Nobody tells you anything unless you persist, and even then you often have to know exactly what to ask. A lot of people fall though the cracks.

It took about three months for my body to get used to the drug and it was pretty rough at first, but I had a lot of help. I really wanted to keep my job, I needed to keep it, but by the time I got home I was just too tired to do all the things a single, working mother has to do, like laundry and grocery shopping and cleaning, not to mention the most important task of all, taking care of my son. Joe was very good about helping me, as was my mom, who came to stay for a while and help out. Even the other girls at work really did a lot for me at work when things got tough.

Eventually I figured out the best way to take it so I would be as functional as possible. Since the symptoms were like having a bad case of the flu, I decided to treat it as such. I don't know about you, but when I get the flu, I take a Tylenol and get into bed.

So that's what I did.

I pre-medicated in the evenings with ibuprofen, and then injected "the flu" before I went to bed. This worked best for me, and I didn't get permission from the doctor first. Again, I didn't want to be taken off the drug, and since I had been told not to deviate from their protocols, I adopted a kind of, don't ask - don't tell policy.

That's now the official protocol, by the way.

During this time, Joe and I were spending more and more time together. He was a lot different from other men I'd been with. He'd never been married and was very straitlaced, and so as a consequence, I became more serious, as well. It's easy to stay out of trouble when you're dating someone who couldn't find trouble with a road map and you live in a dry county. We went to church together, which was nice. Even though I hated Harrisburg, I have to admit that my time there kind of straightened me out.

After my wild bar days that stretched from Long Island to Houston, small town Pennsylvania was a whole new ballgame.

Ironically, my mother didn't like Joe. "He's not for you," she pronounced the first time they met.

You'd think a mother would like a good, church-going suitor for her daughter, but not her. She's a gut instinct kind of person, and she knew it would never work.

My father said the same thing after the big snowstorm.

Joe and I had been dating for a year or so by then, and we made plans to meet in Hawaii over Ryan's winter break from first grade. Joe was traveling in another part of the country. So Ryan and I set out in the car for New York, where my dad was expecting us to stop over before Ryan caught his flight to Texas, and I would go on to Hawaii.

But there was a huge blizzard, and we got caught out on I-78 when they closed the road. We were stuck for hours while the troopers brought all the motorists blankets and snacks, waiting for the weather to clear so they could reopen the highway. This was before everyone had cell phones, so all we could do was wait in the cold. I'm sure my dad probably thought I had done what any sane person would have done and stayed home because of the weather forecast, but I really wanted to get to the beach.

I had bought a new bikini just for the occasion and couldn't wait to show off for my boyfriend.

They finally opened the road, traffic started to move, and then I got lost. Driving conditions were terrible. I stopped the car and tromped up a hill through snowdrifts that were almost up to my neck toward a distant pay phone and called my dad, who confirmed my suspicions that he thought I was out of my mind.

"You'll never get to Hawaii," he said, but there was no turning back.

"I'll get there," I said.

I hadn't waited for hours on the road eating peanuts and drinking stale water to be denied my beach vacation.

We finally made it to the airport. Ryan's flight was rescheduled, but I missed my own flight. I waited in a really long line to get on the next plane, and when I finally got to the ticket counter, I watched as the guy right in front of me snagged the very last seat.

I felt like crying.

All I could think of was how dreary Harrisburg was and how much I wanted to wear that bikini in Hawaii, so I did what any good Catholic girl would do in that situation.

I lied my ass off.

Okay, I may have said a prayer, too, but mostly I lied, I'm ashamed to say. I told the man who'd gotten the last ticket that I was getting married in Maui and I absolutely had to get on that flight. I may have even thrown in a quivering lower lip and a few tears, which by that time were real, and he felt pity on me and gave up his seat.

I was a shit, I know. But I'm hopeful he caught a later flight.

Joe couldn't believe I actually made it, and he proposed to me that very night, with flowers and everything, so it turned out that my lie was almost true. Kind of a pre-lie.

I said yes, and we had a wonderful night together.

And then things got weird.

That new bikini that I bought for the trip? Joe didn't like it at all. I looked really good in it, too, but he just preferred me to wear a one-piece, he said. Then when we got home, he told me that I should quit my job and come to live with him in the house he had in Connecticut.

"What?"

"You don't need to work, now," he said, as if that was all that needed to be said.

But I wanted to work.

"The school district is great," he countered.

"That may be true, but I also need to be somewhere I can get a job."

Joe didn't like that. I was finally discovering just how conservative he was. No bikini I could live with, but no job? No way.

That's when my father chimed in, siding with my mother. "Carol, you're trying to fit a square peg in a round hole," he said, "and it's not gonna work."

Joe didn't even like the clothes I was wearing when we went to my mom's house after our trip, and she noticed that he noticed.

Both my mom and dad knew that Joe was too conservative for me pretty much as soon as they met him, and they were right, of course. Nobody knows you like your parents. They know you better than you know yourself, sometimes.

And that was the end of Joe. If I hadn't bought that bikini, I might've married the guy!

I'm exaggerating, of course. I'm sure I would have eventually come to my senses and realized why we didn't match up. Joe was my serious rebound after my divorce, I suppose. And after everything I'd left behind, I really needed that.

Once our relationship was over, I also really needed to get out of Harrisburg. There was nothing left for me there, but Interstate, Marriott's management company, didn't want to transfer me. I was doing my job too well. They tried to throw money at me, but I told them it didn't matter how much they paid me, I wouldn't stay.

Back to the headhunter.

I had four interviews set up, and found a job with a company in New Jersey that sold blocks of hotel rooms to corporations when they needed temporary, long term lodging for employees, such as when they were building a new branch or facility and needed to set up the business. They paid in advance for lots of rooms at lower level hotels. Technically I would still be working for Interstate, but I'd be under contract to Rooms Unlimited.

It paid well, so I took the job and moved even closer to my roots, this time to West Patterson, New Jersey.

Slowly but surely, I was coming home.

11

R&D and Me

WAS ALSO A LOT CLOSER TO BERLEX LABORATORIES
in Wayne, New Jersey, which was where they were making the
interferon I had come to depend on, so the move was a very cool
thing for me in that regard.

Career-wise, not so much.

I liked my boss, Jeff at Rooms Unlimited, but the job just wasn't all
that interesting to me. I was making good money, but I really missed
just physically being in the hotel. I love hotels. I like the comfort of
them. There's something about a hotel that's calming for me. It's like
a vacation, almost. There's someone to take care of things, a person
for every job. It's all very organized, or at least it should be.

And I liked the actual work that went into running the hotel. There
was always something to keep me busy. It was never boring, believe me.

I'm a problem solver at heart. A nuts and bolts person. Not the
dirty nuts and bolts if I can help it, although I never minded doing
physical labor when I was able.

I mean seeing things that need to get done, and doing them. I like
figuring out ways to make things better. More efficient. Organized.
And I'm good at it. I was good at my job booking the rooms, too, but

having a job you're good at and a job you love, that's what I wanted.

So I was still looking around.

After a year with Rooms Unlimited, I moved to a job at the Madison Hotel in Morristown, NJ, a very high-end hotel with a lot of history. But it was family owned, and I learned pretty quickly never to work for a family owned hotel because a lot of the time they just don't know what they were doing. In this case, the hotel business was secondary to the family after their food and wedding services, and so the job was not all it was cracked up to be.

Interstate lost the contract with them anyway, so they moved me to this disgusting hotel in Newark where I had to step over homeless people on the way to work. It was quite a come down from working in the very elegant Madison Hotel to living in a third floor walkup on skid row. Bums actually lived in the lobby of the hotel, and there was a piano playing all the time to drown out the noise from the subway station down the street. Not a pleasant experience for me.

But I stuck it out.

I only let Ryan come there once, and he was very cute. He took me aside and said in a very serious voice, "Mom, this is not a very nice hotel."

He was concerned for his mother. He was also used to some very fancy hotels at a very early age, and this was definitely not one of them.

Six months later, we lost that contract, too, so things were really falling apart. I was feeling better health-wise since I had connected with the interferon lab, but my career was suddenly going nowhere.

It's always something.

But I always land on my feet, and I was hired through Prime

Hospitality as director of sales and marketing at the Radisson, where I had a much larger staff than ever before and a lot more responsibility. I also had a female general manager, which was both unusual for the time and one of the reasons I took the job. There may have been three other female GMs in the entire country. Even today, there are probably twice as many males in that job as females. The people who own hotels like to hire pretty girls in sales and let the men hang back and actually run things. Typical.

It was a good move for me. Ellen Sinclair was a wonderful boss, very patient as I learned the more difficult computer system and got used to managing more people. She had faith in me from day one, which is always a confidence builder. She was very encouraging as I found my way, and helpful in every way. She even encouraged me to buy a house in the area, and gave me some good advice. And if I was tied up with work and Ryan needed to be picked up from school, she just sent one of the bellmen to pick him up and bring him to the hotel.

"They're just sitting on their asses, anyway," she said, which was true a lot of the time. Ellen was great. She was a problem solver, too.

Ryan loved it, of course. He was like Little Lord Fauntleroy, being ushered around by men in uniform and running around fancy hotels. The bellmen thought he was a hoot, and Ellen loved having him around, too.

But like all good things, it didn't last. I should have figured Ellen wouldn't stay, because she was very sharp and would of course go on to bigger and better things.

So I had been there six months, had a great job and a great boss, just closed on a house, set up a real support network through friends and neighbors that I'd met, and then Ellen told me the news. She'd taken a terrific job with AT&T as a vice president.

I was crushed.

She told me before she told the Radisson.

"Listen Carol," she told me, "there are going to be a lot of people that want this job. They're like vultures. But corporate will take their time, so a lot of this will be on you."

"What?"

"You can do this job, Carol. You know you can."

There was something in the way she said that which immediately gave me the confidence I needed. She was right, I could do the job. She had been a great teacher. It was no big deal.

"There's one more thing."

"What's that?" I asked, already envisioning myself in her office, taking charge.

"We're starting renovations next month."

So I would be running a major hotel without a GM during the renovation of three hundred and fifty-four rooms.

That was a very big deal.

So Ellen left for her dream job, and corporate was also very supportive, or at least they started out that way. I was told not to worry about the renovations, that the workers knew what to do and didn't need supervising.

"They'll take care of everything."

Yeah, right.

These guys were typical New Jersey construction workers, always late and hung over. Especially the construction supervisor, a Guido-type character named Joe with coffee breath and a bad attitude. Just the kind of guy I wanted to fight with every day about the noise and the disruption to the guests that they were supposed to be avoiding.

I was miserable with this guy. I was on the phone to corporate every day complaining, but they did nothing. They basically paid me lip service and expected me to handle it. What did they care? We were at 100% occupancy!

Except for whatever floor the workers were renovating, which meant that my bonus was affected because thirty-three rooms were out of commission. I thought I should have gotten credit for those rooms since they couldn't be sold, but the corporate formula said otherwise, and I was not happy.

Not only were these guys slow, they were stupid. One day I just caught them before the geniuses were about to cut one of the new bathtubs in half because they couldn't fit it through the door to the room!

What they were going to do with it after that, I have no idea. I couldn't understand why they bought tubs that wouldn't fit in the first place.

I dealt with this situation for a year. Constant fights with Joe the Plumber, little help from corporate, three am wake up calls when the fire alarm would go off because those idiots were heating roofing tar too close to a sensor or something, after which the fire marshal would order the evacuation of the entire hotel as a precaution (and didn't the hotel guests love that).

It was always something.

The roofing tar set off the alarm four nights in a row. It was insane. We got a citation every time, too.

I learned from that, however. On the fifth night, a guy in one of the older rooms with a kitchenette actually set off the alarm for real, so I

called Peter from corporate in the middle of the night and made him
meet me at the hotel and help me go door-to-door through the entire
hotel to convince the guests that this time was the real deal. None of
them believed any of the regular hotel staff telling them to leave and
were slamming the door in their faces.

Ryan loved it. He came with me and was running around banging
on doors like a champ. He actually took it very seriously, which was
adorable.

He also helped me with lobby lizard duty.

This is something every hotel has. At seven in the morning, the
hotel guests start to leave for the day, maybe grabbing coffee before
catching the shuttle, so someone had to be there at six-thirty and be
ready to greet them as they left.

That someone is the lobby lizard.

Everyone was on rotation so they didn't have to do it every day,
but it still sucked. Out of all the employees, maybe forty could look
presentable and function at that hour of the morning without scaring
the guests, so it was not a frequent duty, but I showed up once or twice
a week to set a good example, even though I was the boss.

Ryan also loved the weddings. It was a very pretty hotel, and we
hosted a lot of weddings. Ryan would go up to the bride and offer to
carry her things, which everyone thought was so cute, and he made
a lot of tips that way.

He's also in the wedding pictures of more strangers than a justice
of the peace.

If he got sick I would keep home from school and put him in one of
the empty rooms and let him order room service, which he loved, and
he learned to do a lot of hotel-like duties like rollups for the restaurant,

putting the silverware in the napkins, and other things. He knew that hotel like the back of his hand by the time he was ten. It was like the world's greatest clubhouse to him. He was in heaven.

As for me, I was having a rough time. After the bathtub incident, Peter from corporate finally read Joe the Plumber the riot act and I got a little more respect from his crew, but health-wise, it was a struggle.

The stress had been unbelievable, and it was really hitting me hard. I didn't have a full-blown attack, but I was very fatigued, and even started to have cognitive problems. I had to forecast future sales, we're talking millions of dollars of revenues versus expenditures, and I just couldn't concentrate. I had to slow down to get it right and the report would take me twice as long as normal. But I couldn't afford any mistakes with those numbers involved.

I was fortunate because since Berlex Labs, which is no owned by Bayer, was so close, they would often book our conference rooms for some of their meetings. I would sit in, of course, because they were talking about interferon. I learned a lot from that, and then got a great idea.

I called their meeting planner and asked her to lunch. Her name was Kathy Walter, and that meeting changed my life.

When I told her about my MS and my situation, she said I was exactly what they were looking for.

"I know," I said.

They had been planning to spin off a new support program for patients on interferon, but because they had always been so focused on selling the drug and not the person actually using the drug, they had no idea what they were doing.

"I know," I said.

All of those meetings really paid off.

I was like a fountain of actual, real world experience for her. I knew the doctors because I'd been chasing them down for so long and picking their brains, and I knew the patients because I was one.

"What you're telling your salespeople isn't going to go over very well with anyone," I told her, and then I explained why.

For example, they were basically training their sales force to sell the drug to the doctors, who would then sell the drug to the patients. But the doctors didn't have the education to explain to the patients how to deal with the drug once they got it, which meant they were totally dependent on the patients just blindly accepting what their doctor said without much to back it up.

People will only do that for so long before they demand more, and most people won't go to all the trouble I did to come up with protocols on my own. A lot of them will just suffer through it and maybe even die.

I was filled with ideas because having gone through all of it, I knew what would have made things easier for me. The doctors needed to be able to tell patients what I had to discover on my own. There needed to be a hotline for patients to call in a crisis, or even with a simple question, which is standard operating procedure now but had not been set up back then.

Who calls their doctor at home with a simple question at four in the morning? Who calls their doctor at home at all? And who could the doctor call when they had a question?

Berlex needed to develop protocols the doctor could use to help the patient get the best results with their medication. It's just sales with an eye on future sales. You want to keep the customer happy so they keep coming back.

So we did all that, and it was a revelation.

They didn't even realize that patients responded better to nurses than to the doctors, in many cases.

For example, the doctor is the one who breaks the bad news. He tells you that you have an incurable disease, and that your life is never going to be the same. Then he gives you the name of the drug and tells you how to use it, and sends you home.

First of all, as I've explained, the doctors don't really know how to use the drug, because knowing how to use a drug also means knowing how not to use it. Interferon can be a dangerous medication if you do a certain thing, and it can be dangerous if don't do something else.

Meanwhile, the patient goes home and forgets everything the doctor said after the words, "You have an incurable disease."

That's literally the only thing you remember.

You can see the problem.

So I told her that patients need support. And who provides support?

Nurses. Nurses are like the angels, and doctors are like God. Doctors are absolute. Intimidating. Patients can get scared of doctors. They're so busy, you don't want to take up their time, etc. They come in and out of the room and before you know it, they're gone.

Whereas nurses are there. Helpful and kind. At least they should be, and to be honest, I have known some nurses who are one step removed from saints. It is such a hard job, and they deal with such terrible problems, and some of them are so incredibly helpful. They are an inspiration.

I've seen a few bitches, too.

But mostly, it's a profession that deserves and receives a lot of respect from me. I would never call it a thankless job because I thanked them all the time, and you should, too, if you deal with them. A nurse may save your life one day. Or they may just quietly do their job taking your vital signs or administering care as needed.

Plus, you gossip with the nurses. You call them over and tell them your problems, and most of the time they actually listen. They might even tell you a few secrets of their own. You can confide in a nurse.

So I told Kathy that the nurses had to be involved. I knew that doctors palm off a lot of things on their nurse, anyway, so we might as well educate them both.

And it went like that the entire lunch. I talked and she listened, and it was really a wonderful thing for us both. She was finally hearing from an actual patient, and I had finally found someone in a position to help who would also actually listen to all of my problems and suggestions.

As they say down in Texas and probably a lot of other places, I talked her ear off.

She was so excited that she insisted I repeat everything I told her to Wolfgang.

"Who's Wolfgang?"

"He's the president of operations."

And that was how I went to work for the company that made interferon.

12

Trailblazing

DID NOT, HOWEVER, LEAVE MY JOB. AS I SAID, I LOVE the hotel business. But I was able to do much like I did down in Houston, which was to use my medical contacts to increase my business with the hotel.

I offered to help them in exchange for all their meetings at my hotel, or as many as we could handle, and there were going to be a lot of meetings. The company had seven drugs at the time, and I knew about all of them before I met with Wolfgang. And I knew if they were going to set up new protocols and create a new patient support system with the twenty-four hour hotline to go with it, it was going to require a lot of training for a lot of people.

And that was good for my business.

I also knew going in how many meetings and conferences they booked annually with other hotels.

Kathy was impressed. "How do you know all that?" She asked me.

"They're my competitors," I answered. "Of course I know what my competitors are selling."

At that point they could see that I had come to do some business.

I told Wolfgang that I was sure my company would be more than happy to "loan me out" to help train their people since we were getting so much new business, and I could see the wheels turning. He was a businessman, and I had just offered him up my services on someone else's dime that was going to increase his business, and all he had to do was a little cost shifting. They had to meet somewhere, why not the Radisson?

It was a match made in heaven, and a deal was struck. Not immediately; he took a little time to think about it. He had that German way about him, very analytical, but he came to same conclusion I did, that it would be a win-win, and drew up some contracts.

I would have helped them anyway, of course, at least as much as I could. What I went through with the meds in the early days was hard, and if I could help others avoid that, I was just paying it forward.

But this way, I could devote a lot more time to it because the Radisson was still paying me. It was also good for my health, because as I've related, although I love the hotel business, it could get stressful. And stress is bad. On the other hand, I also love helping people, and helping people eases my stress. It's good for the soul.

Now, it wasn't strictly a no-cost proposition for Berlex. After all, this was a strictly regulated drug in a highly regulated industry. They had to pay something so it would not be considered an inducement, so they paid me an honorarium. A very decent honorarium. And they flew me all over the country. I gave talks to their people, relating my experiences on their drug, and how they could better help their patients.

I also had it in my contract that whenever possible, Ryan could come along. He was my guy, and I wanted him with me as much as possible, plus if I left him at home, I had to hire someone to stay with him. It helped that I became very good friends with Kathy and one of her colleagues, a woman named Cindy, and we all had kids, so we bonded over that and looked out for each other the way that mothers do.

That's why more women need to be in charge of things. We can be just as tough as men when we have to be, but there's something about being a mother, carrying a child inside you and then giving birth to a tiny human being and nursing that baby that gives you a special capacity for empathy. Not that men don't empathize, of course they do. But with women, it's innate. Men are protectors; women are nurturers. We each learn the role of the other, but I think a lot of men in positions of power could use more of that nurturing side.

So I took Ryan with me as much as I could, and he was a great little traveler. That kid was flying as an unaccompanied minor from the time he was five years old, if you can believe that, and he was a real trooper. He'd flown back and forth to Texas to see his dad from an early age, and now he was flying all over the country with me.

The first time Ryan went with me on one of my big trips, we arrived at the convention center in Chicago and he was totally shocked when we walked in and right there was a twelve by twelve foot booth with a life size cutout of me in front of it. I was on all the boxes and promotional materials, too.

He stopped in his tracks and looked at me with awe. "Mom, you're famous!"

It was a surprise to me, too, actually. I didn't know I was going to be their spokes model! It was funny because for a year or two you couldn't go into a neurologist's office without seeing my smiling face.

What I was really happy about was that hotline. Twenty-four

seven, people with MS could call and get help. And now interferon had competitors; two new drugs were being developed to treat MS. And because we set the bar with that hotline that meant the other drug companies did the same. And you could also connect with other patients and actually talk to someone who was going through what you were going through. Totally different from when I was diagnosed, and so much better.

It made me very happy to be a tiny part of that, and hopeful for the future.

My mother even went with me on a cruise ship conference. They were following us around with a camera crew for a video on MS, and my mother played the role of herself quite beautifully. She didn't care much for the entourage, but she managed. Better still, I think it really helped her better understand what MS is and what it does.

It's always been a mysterious disease to a certain extent. It's hard to understand someone who looks healthy but suddenly can't move their legs. Or someone who goes blind with no warning. It's hard to convey unless you experience it yourself, but now my mother probably understands it as well as anyone who's not afflicted, and that helps a lot.

Everybody needs to be understood.

We had a lot of fun on that trip, too. My mother's a character.

The MS Foundation held the event once a year, called Cruise for the Cause, and I gave a talk that year like I had done many times before, which was basically just telling my story. What it was like to be diagnosed, how I felt, and things like that. Then there would be a Q and A.

I think those question and answer sessions helped my mother see me in an entirely new light. I was humbled when one of the doctors came up to me and told me that they wouldn't have known a lot of things they knew without my help, and my mother was standing there beside me. I think she was very proud of me at that moment, and I liked that feeling very much.

I did the event seven years in a row, and I always got a lot out of it. I really liked talking to the other people with MS after the talks. It was very moving to see them and hear their stories, and very gratifying that I could help them in my own small way.

I was still with Radisson, of course, and I did occasionally stay home and do my actual job. In spite of my heavy workload and all the stress, I only had one full-blown attack while I worked there. And once again, God showed me the way to make lemonade out of lemons.

It was 1998 and I started to have trouble with my balance and was getting double vision. I drove myself to the hospital, which I definitely should not have done, and by the time I got there I was even having trouble speaking. I knew what I wanted to say, but the words came out garbled. As many times as this happened, it was still always a very scary experience.

They admitted me immediately.

The next day, I began to hemorrhage pretty badly. It was terrible. I couldn't just have an MS attack, I had to also have the world's worst period at the same time. At least I was in the hospital.

Of course, it's all related. The stress of the attack made it worse.

They gave me steroids for inflammation in my brain, but the steroids kept me awake, so I was constantly getting up all night, which was very bad. I was supposed to stay off my feet, because if my legs gave out or something I could hurt myself. But I couldn't just lay there awake all night, so I got up.

Bad move. The hemorrhaging was so bad that I was lightheaded, and of course I did fall, right on my face, splitting my lip open and losing even more blood.

The nurse ran in and started screaming for help, but I was already unconscious. I'm sure I was a sight, laying on the floor and bleeding all over the place.

It was just horrendous.

So now on top of the MS attack, on top of the period from hell, now I look like the Bride of Frankenstein or something with my stitched up face.

After that, they put an alarm on me.

My friends who came to see me were horrified. I was a mess. I couldn't walk, it was hard to breathe, my face is all beat up, and I was practically strapped to the bed to keep me down even though I could barely walk, anyway. It was a nightmare.

I got through it, but when I got home, it was obvious that I was going to need some help. I was using a walker, and that was just not me, but you do what you have to do. My insurance paid for part time help, but with Ryan that wasn't going to be enough.

Once again, my life was going to change pretty drastically.

I didn't know when they released me, but it would be another three or four months before I could walk again. I had a lot of rehab in front of me.

I went on long-term disability. There really was nothing else I could do. But once you do that, it's the beginning of the end. It's a red flag to an employer. They knew and I knew that I wasn't getting any better.

Sooner or later, they would find a way to get rid of me, and I understood that, so I started to make plans to move on and I'm sure they started to make plans to ease me out. It's just business, except that for me, of course, it was also my life. But I accepted that. I had been through a lot, and something had always presented itself as an opportunity to enable me to move past whatever obstacle I found in front of me. I accepted it because what else could I do?

It's always something.

So my employer and I began circling each other with a wary eye, both of us trying to find an advantage. You can't just fire a contracted employee for getting sick when she was sick when you hired her, especially while she was on long-term disability. I knew they would try and figure out a way to get me back in and then get me out legally, and the fact was that they didn't want me or need me there full time, anyway. By that point, they had adapted to me being away with my MS work and enjoyed the fruits of my association in the form of all those bookings. And I knew that I couldn't stay on disability forever. So it was all going to end.

It was just a matter of when and how.

As always, the good Lord smiled on me, and this time He presented an opportunity in the form of my dependable sister Joanne, who got me a position with a small Internet start-up no one had ever heard of by the name of WebMD.

This was 1998, remember.

Joanne had worked at Variety, the film industry magazine out in Los Angeles, and one of her friends, Katherine Silver, had left the magazine to start this new web site for medical information with a friend in Atlanta. She knew about my experience with Berlex, now Bayer, and asked if I was feeling up to a new job helping them out with this new idea of theirs.

"Katherine, I don't know anything about the Internet," I said.

"Nobody does!" She laughed. "But they will."

She was a very confident person, a real go-getter. When Katherine wanted to do something, she just went out and did it.

I said okay.

My job would be to go to institutions like universities who collected medical data and somehow convince them to share that information with us so we could put it on the Internet.

In 1998.

Nowadays everything's on the Internet; people live their lives on the Internet, but imagine going to some place like Duke University back then and asking them to share all the information they've been compiling for years and years so that you can try and make money off it by putting it on the Internet for everyone to see, when they didn't understand the Internet any better than you did.

Who would you even ask?

But that's what I was going to do.

Before I started, however, I had to get better.

I did rehab every day. My family, as they have always been, were incredibly supportive. I could not have gotten through that time without them. Ryan was also great about helping me. He never got scared, although seeing his mother like that could not have been easy. Ryan just went to school and did his thing and then came home and helped me out. He was such an amazing kid, and still is.

Once I was ready to start traveling again, Katherine sent me out into the world. She really had no special guidance for me other than to go out and get those agreements to share the information. She couldn't even really explain to me how exactly how it was all going to work, because I don't think she knew, herself. But she was going to double my salary, so I wasn't complaining.

The Internet was wide open and we were mostly making it up as we went along.

Once again, I was blazing my own trail with more than a little help from the man upstairs and a lot of people who had loved and supported me all my life, and continue to do so to this day. This has been my existence. A lot of bumps in the road and a lot of help from family and friends to get over them. I have been blessed in that regard.

There were other big changes happening, as well.

Around this time I met a guy named Joe, and before too long he'd moved in with Ryan and me and I was imagining myself married to this sweet little Italian guy in his nice little Italian neighborhood, with absolutely no idea of the dangerous secrets he was harboring in his dark little Italian heart.

But that's another chapter.

13

Hardball

JOE WAS MY HAIRDRESSER AND HE WAS MY BOY-
friend. Or I should say that I had my hair done at his salon. He
didn't actually cut my hair. Joe was a very friendly, gregarious
guy, and very Italian.

I had been renting the house across the street from his salon while
I was with Radisson, and if you know anything about what it takes for
a woman to maintain that "naturally highlighted" look, then you can
guess how much time I spent at Joe's salon!

Also, a hair salon is always information central in small towns, and
all my friends knew that I was looking for a house to buy. I was ready
to put down some roots.

Joe was married at the time and there was nothing romantic
implied or inferred, but he was one of those expansive, helpful guys.
He was like the mayor of this very close-knit Italian neighborhood.
Joe knew everybody and everybody knew Joe, and half of them were
related in some way. It was a great place to live and everybody looked
out for each other.

Everybody also knew everybody's business, too, or at least they
thought they did, but it wasn't intrusive or anything. If you wanted

to be left alone, they left you alone. If you wanted to gossip a little bit, well, that was fine, too. My neighborhood growing up was like that. People are the same all over. On the whole, it was a very nice place for me and my son to be.

I finally found a house about a mile from where I'd been renting and bought it in 1998. Joe brought me a big welcome basket with wine and pasta and told me to let him know if I needed anything. That's the kind of guy he was, or I should say, that was the side he revealed to me.

The house was tiny, what a realtor would call cozy, with a second kitchen, what Italians call a summer kitchen, which was located on the lower floor, what most people call a basement.

It was what I called a potential studio rental. All it needed was a bathroom.

Joe recommended a few guys who could do the plumbing work to complete the little apartment, but I found someone cheaper, a big, quiet Persian guy, who also ended up becoming my first tenant. But he also became what one of the local wise guys would call a slow pay, and suddenly I had every landlord's nightmare: A tenant who wouldn't pay or leave.

Joe came to my rescue. When I told him about my problem, he told me to take Ryan out for some ice cream.

"Joe, I don't need ice cream, I need to figure out what to do about this guy."

"Take your son out for a cone and I'll have a talk with him."

I just looked at Joe. My tenant was a big guy. Joe was a small guy. I shrugged.

"Okay."

I left with Ryan and we walked down the street to get ice cream, and when we got back, my tenant was gone. Not only that, all of his things were gone. There was no trace of his existence.

We had been gone a half an hour, tops.

"Joe, what did you say to him?"

Joe just smiled.

This should have been my first clue that there was more to Joe than I realized, but I was so happy to have the guy gone I didn't give it much more thought. Maybe Joe was just a real convincing guy.

I didn't find out until later that one of the reasons Joe was such a convincing guy was that he was also a connected guy. What the cops would call a criminal, or "part of the family."

The whole neighborhood was, I just didn't know it at the time. I mean, this neighborhood was so Italian, people made their own wine. When your bottles were empty, you'd just leave them out on the curb and they would be picked up and refilled by the next day. That's Italian.

Because everybody was connected, that made it a very safe neighborhood. I was oblivious to it all at first, but everybody was involved at keeping things nice and quiet. For example, my next-door neighbor Helen would take down the license plates of any unfamiliar cars that came into the neighborhood. One day I got a call from the police captain down at our precinct.

"You know this guy Steve Manzoni?"

"Uh, yeah. We went out last night."

"Well, he's married."

"What?!"

"Don't worry. You won't see him around anymore."

"Uh, thanks."

It was hysterical.

Once when I let my grass get a little high, Mr. Constantino from across the street knocked on my door.

"Anything wrong?"

"No, why?"

"Your yard's looking a little …" and he made that sketchy motion with his hand.

"Oh, that," I laughed. "I've been a little tired lately."

"Tell you what. I'm gonna send over a gardener."

"Mister Constantino, you don't have to do that."

"I'm a take care of it. You relax with your boy, don't worry about nothin.'"

That afternoon, a crew came over and did a beautiful job on my lawn, and kept it up for a month. The fifth week, this polite middle-aged man knocked on my door.

"Are you happy with the work? On the lawn?"

"Oh, yes, thank you so much!"

"You want us to keep goin'?"

"How much do you charge?"

"How much you wanna pay?"

I just looked at him. He was very nice, but it sounded a little weird to me. His crew had been cutting my lawn for a month, the guy should know what he would charge.

"Well, how much would you charge me?"

"I'm not supposed to say."

"What do you mean, you're not supposed to say?"

"I'm just supposed to say, 'how much can you pay?' "

I laughed. "Oh, I don't know…thirty dollars?" It was low. I had a big lawn.

"Thirty dollars." He nodded, tipped his cap, and left.

And that was that.

The cops and the criminals all got along, and nobody bothered anyone who lived there. Most of the cops were probably on the take, to be honest, and the connected guys would never bring trouble into their neighborhood. So there was an understanding.

I got along well with everyone. I worked on a lot of fundraisers for the cops, actually. I was very organized, and whenever the West Patterson PD needed to plan an event, say to raise money for the family of a slain officer, I would set it up and the whole neighborhood would turn out and support it.

It was a great place to raise a kid, and I never worried about Ryan.

As a matter of fact, it was almost impossible for him to get into any trouble. The poor kid couldn't sneeze without me hearing about it. The whole police force knew him from the fundraisers, so if he so much as lit up a cigarette down at the mall, it was like a SWAT team would descend on him.

"You know your mother don't want you smokin', right?"

"Yes, sir."

"Put it out."

"Yes, sir."

"Atta boy."

Everybody knew Ryan.

About six weeks after Joe took care of my problem tenant, I got a phone bill for over six thousand dollars. Apparently the guy was part of some terror cell in the Middle East and had been calling Saudi Arabia and other places, so it was a very big deal with the FBI in the house and haggling with AT&T. This was before 9/11, but it was a very scary thing. I have no idea whatever happened to my tenant after that, but who knows?

I called Joe and thanked him once more for getting the guy out of my hair.

"Speaking of hair, when are you coming in for yours?" He joked.

"I'll be in soon, I promise."

"You know, my wife, I think we're splitting up."

I had heard she was cheating on him and planning to divorce him.

"Joe, I'm so sorry to hear that."

"What can you do?"

That was Joe's way of telling me that he thought I was attractive and he was coming onto the market soon, and I read him loud and clear. Joe was a pretty handsome guy, and don't think I hadn't noticed.

Eventually his wife did leave him, and we started dating. I was working at WebMD, and traveling quite a bit, and the closer Joe and I got, the more it looked like this could be my life. I was good with that.

Joe adored Ryan, like everybody else who met him, and Ryan really took to Joe, too. Joe even started staying with Ryan when I was out of town, and became almost like a second father to him. Or at least a man he looked up to and trusted.

Which made what eventually happened all the more painful.

But for a while, things were really good. Joe eventually moved in with me, he was crazy about my kid, and I was making a lot of money.

What could go wrong?

There's always something.

Actually, the truth was that Joe was in love with me, and he wanted to marry me, but I wasn't ready. "I don't know you well enough," I said, which turned out to be truer than I realized. Boy, did I not know Joe. Thank God we didn't get married.

But I'll get to that later.

Anyway, I had my job with WebMD, the pharmaceutical company for their promotional events was paying me, and I was being paid for the fundraisers I organized, which had now expanded into the political world.

I was a busy girl.

Too busy. It really was too much. I had to be in Atlanta on every Monday and Friday, which I thought was crazy but my bosses insisted I at least check in. So I might travel to the west coast to visit UCLA Medical Center on Monday, fly back to Tennessee and Vanderbilt midweek, then head back to the home office in Atlanta on Friday to turn in all my paperwork and finish my reports, then fly home for the weekend and start all over again on Monday. It was exhausting.

But it was also exhilarating. We were doing what nobody had ever done before with medical records technology. And the deals were amazing. Huge money. I was also meeting some amazing people. I had an unlimited expense account, so the partners all loved me. This was all back in the dial-up days, too, so all of the Internet stuff was evolving right in front of me. I loved it.

All that travel was kicking my ass, though, and I had a major attack on an escalator in the Charlotte airport. A guy standing a couple of steps below caught me after I lost my vision and just collapsed. If he hadn't have been there, I probably would have tumbled right down the escalator and broken my neck.

This guy was such a sweet man. He followed my ambulance to the hospital and his wife brought me dinner later that night. They were really something. God bless southern hospitality.

I was released from the hospital a couple of days later, and then I went home.

A lot of things were happening back there, too.

WebMD had just recently public, and Jim Clark, the founder of Netscape, kind of came in to clean house. He'd started a company called Healtheon a few years before to do some of the same things we were doing, but we were a little further along, so they joined forces.

The scuttlebutt was that the days of unlimited expense accounts and giving out computers like candy and all the rest of it had to brought under control, and some heads would roll.

I was just hoping mine wouldn't be one of them.

Once you go public, everything changes, and people were scrambling. We had a company with too many chiefs and not enough Indians to do the actual work, and that couldn't continue.

Like everyone else, I was freaking out. It seemed like every time I found a great job and got settled, something went wrong. Katherine, the girl who had brought me in, was no help to me at all.

"You? Who cares what happens to you? I'm going to sue the bastards."

Thanks for your support!

She wasn't the only one talking about suing, either. Rumors were rampant, and I had no idea what was going to happen. Once again, I had been sailing along, full speed ahead, and hit a big bump in the road.

It's always something.

In spite of my doubts regarding marriage, Joe had been incredibly supportive through all that. As a matter of fact, there was no way I could have even done the job without him. With all that travel? Him staying with Ryan was a Godsend. Not to mention, he was hot. I had no doubts about that.

I think I mentioned that, right?

During this time, Joe had a few things going on, too, although I had no idea about some of it. He'd gotten his divorce, which was kind of nasty, he had to sell both his house and the shop because his wife was half owner, and there was a lot of family stuff. He had a big falling out with his brother, his mother sided against him and for the brother, the brother went in business with his ex-wife, it was big, typical Italian mess.

So we depended on each other, and we got closer because of it. You bond with someone in tough times, and times were tough.

With all of the turmoil at work, I was worried it would be like before, when Radisson tried to get rid of me because I'd gotten sick. That experience taught me a lot, so in whatever dealings I had with HR, I always took meticulous notes and made sure they were aware of everything that was going on with me.

Sure enough, they called me in and told me that since there were so many changes at the company, I should just take a buy out and leave since I had been out sick a lot, anyway.

It's always the same. I am very pro-business, but the business community has a lot to learn about taking care of their people. I was their best salesperson and had brought in an awful lot of money for them. I was one of those worker bees that put them where they were.

Speaking of which, I had four deals hanging at that very moment which meant over sixty million dollars in the first two years alone, a percentage of which was mine.

As the neighborhood wise guys would say, they owed me a taste.

No way was I taking their package, and I told them so.

They tried to play hardball with me, another habit of businesses when you're sick. They think they can take advantage of you when you're in a weakened. But I was ready for that. They had never given an employee handbook that spelled everything out, and I'd been asking for a while. It was required under the law, but they always had some excuse.

And I had my notes of every single encounter and every single conversation. If I bumped into someone from HR coming out of the ladies room, I wrote it down.

But they lied and pressured and did their worst, but I would not sign their separation papers. They fired me two days after I went to see an attorney.

We ended up in mediation, and because I knew what I was doing and they didn't, I came out of it okay. But from the time I had the attack until the mediation was over, it was seven or eight months, which made for a very stressful year for me, which in turn only made my health problems worse. It was hell.

It had helped me that they were so disorganized. For example, after my attack I'd gone to them and asked about short-term disability, and their response was just, 'don't worry about it, just stay on salary.'

So technically they had no claim that I had been missing work at all, which meant it was a lot tougher for them to claim I had been missing work. I think there were sixty lawsuits and they went into mediation with everybody, but no one had as much documentation as I did.

My mediation took four days, and in the end I got a nice settlement and five years of COBRA insurance, which was really important, obviously. They also paid my legal fees, which my attorney donated to MS charities. I was very moved by that.

Finally, I could breath again. Everything seemed like it was going to be okay.

Then Joe needed to borrow some money and I had another bad attack, and everything was chaos again. Out of the frying pan and into the fire.

It's always something.

14

Never Again

IT WAS OBVIOUS THAT I WAS NEVER GOING TO BE ABLE to work again, at least in the way I always had. And I accepted that, but it was hard. I'd been working since I was a teenager, and so this was a very big milestone in my life. I knew the day would come eventually; I mean I'd been told I couldn't work when I was first diagnosed and many times thereafter, but I loved to work and I have always just done what I wanted to do, for the most part. So I had always kind of put those thoughts away and just went about my life, hoping the day would never come.

The day came.

I got really sick after I left WebMD, and the doctors said that was enough. They told me I just couldn't keep doing what I was doing, and I would never function at the same level again. It was just too much strain on my body.

They found four new lesions on my brain, which gave me a grand total of sixteen. When I first started, there were three.

Brain lesions are basically scars that affect the neurons that carry electrical impulses, which tell other parts of your body what to do. That's why my legs would stop working or I would go blind. And since stress caused the lesions to form and my work was causing stress, it was time to stop. I could go blind permanently, or my spine could get hit and then I'd be in a wheelchair for the rest of my life.

Now, some people with MS have no lesions and have a hard time and others have a lot of them and do fine. MS can affect different people in different ways. For me, the growing number of lesions was a very bad sign.

So even though I had spent many years doing what the doctors told me I shouldn't do, this time I decided to take their advice.

I applied for Medicare and SSDI, which is Social Security Disability Insurance. And of course, dealing with government agencies is its own special brand of hell, which was stressful in and of itself. That's the thing about health insurance. Just dealing with all that stuff can make whatever you got, worse.

A lot of people use an attorney to apply for SSDI, who does all the paperwork and once you're approved, they take a percentage of your first year's payment, but my attorney on the WebMD settlement told me to just do it myself.

"Carol, you know this stuff better than anyone, so why give up the money?"

And it was true. I did it all myself and got approved on the first try because my MRI looked so bad. I had heard rumors that they routinely denied first claims and you'd have to reapply, but I sailed right through. Medicare would not start for two years, though, so if I had not had COBRA insurance coverage, I would have been screwed.

Even with insurance, it was expensive.

And of course, the government agreed that I was disabled, but they automatically make you wait two years before they give you medical coverage. I told the woman assigned to my case that it sounded like they were just hoping I'd die.

"You didn't hear that from me," she said, and went back to her computer screen. But it was done.

So I'd spent the last year trying to save my job, fighting the corporate lawyers, going through mediation, dealing with government bureaucracy, and then Joe tells me he needs a loan because otherwise he and his brother could lose their beauty shop.

It's always something.

So I loaned him the money, but I insisted on looking at the books because I considered this an investment in the business. Only they had no books. They had scraps of paper in a shoebox. Napkins. Photocopies of receipts with lasagna stains.

It was a mess. And his brother hadn't paid their taxes for five years.

There was a lot of cash going through the business that had not been declared, so again, maybe I should have suspected that Joe was not exactly above board in all his dealings, but I really thought that was his family more than him. There were more surprises to come, however.

I managed to get them straightened out with a little help from some friends, but I made sure not to put my name on anything. I may have been a little naïve, but I wasn't stupid. So my investment was basically just an uncollateralized loan.

In the meantime, I went to beauty school to learn how to do facials, and then took a space in their shop and took the monthly rent I would have paid off what they owed. Things seemed to be working out.

Joe and I were a pretty good team. A lot of local movers and shakers like judges and state senators and businessmen would come in on Saturday mornings and Joe would give them a straight edge shave, send them upstairs to me, I would do a men's facial, and then Joe would cut their hair. When they asked how much, I just said, "whatever Joe said," and without fail they'd give me a hundred dollars.

They always asked me after I was done, too. Never before.

I met quite a few guys who were in the sanitation business, if you know what I mean. They had lots of money.

I couldn't work all the time because I would get tired, but I could do maybe four facials a day, three days a week.

Joe was still after me to get married, but I told him know. Now it wasn't that I needed to get to know him better, it was that I knew him a little too much. Don't get me wrong, I loved Joe. He was a great guy to me, very romantic, he got along great with Ryan, and I loved his family. We had a lot of good times. But there was something about him that just made me a little wary. Going to his family gatherings was like a Soprano family picnic. For his 50th birthday party, there was a cake in the shape of a machine gun. My sister couldn't believe it. I couldn't believe it.

But that was how they were, with the big hair and the vaguely suspicious cousins, and it was all a little bit much. Joe laughed it off and I trusted him. He wasn't responsible for what they did any more than I had been responsible for my cousin down in Texas showing up on the local version of Cops, right? So while maybe I didn't know the whole truth about Joe, I at least knew enough not to make that commitment.

Best decision of my life.

It turned out that a lot of things had been happening at my house with Joe when I wasn't around, and it had been going on for a long time.

Jerry Speziale was the sheriff of Passaic County, and I had done a lot of work with him on fundraisers and things. For example, he had this carnival for disadvantaged kids, and I did the PR for him, things like that.

We got along great, and he was a very cool guy, a former undercover DEA agent in New York who helped bring down some major drug cartel kingpins back in the 90's. He eventually wrote a book about it, and he's been on TV a lot to talk about crime and things like that. Now I think he works for the Port Authority.

Anyway, one night I got a call from Jerry, and he was very serious, not joking around at all.

"Carol, I'm sorry to have to tell you this, but your boyfriend is not a good guy."

"Jerry," I said, "I know about his family."

"Not his family, Carol. Him."

So Jerry gave me a tip off that the next day, this guy Skippy was going to be wearing an orange jump suit. He was going to be arrested for drug trafficking, and it wasn't going to be pretty. It would be all over the news, too.

"So what does that have to do with Joe?"

"It's his best friend, Carol."

"I know, but - "

"Trust me, Carol."

"So when is this going to happen?" I asked.

"It's happening right now."

"I don't understand..."

"Carol, Skippy's been in your house."

"What are you talking about?" The way he said it was just so ominous.

Apparently Skippy and Joe had been meeting in my house and doing God know what while I was gone, and Jerry wanted me to know that it was only a matter of time before my house was searched, too. Skippy was connected to Joe and Joe was connected to me, and Jerry didn't want to see me involved in what was going to be an ugly business. I mean, I knew Skippy was kind of shady and figured some of Joe's family was, too, but I really thought Joe was okay. Until that very moment, I believed him when he told me he wasn't a part of all that. I loved him, so I believed him.

You sleep in the same bed with someone and you share your secrets with them, and you think they're sharing theirs with you, but it ain't necessarily so.

"Get him out of your house tonight, Carol. And all his shit, too."

Jerry was all business. He wouldn't be telling me that unless it was pretty serious, so I thanked him, hung up the phone, and sent Ryan across the street to the Constantino's.

Suddenly I had a very bad feeling.

I went downstairs to where I used the rent the room, which was where Joe kept some of his things. I hadn't even been down there for a long time.

There were all kinds of boxes in the closet, stuff I didn't even want to see. Lots of stuff that fell off a truck somewhere instead of being offloaded at Macy's. That kind of thing and worse.

I called Joe. "Joe, you need to come home right now."

"I'm busy right now."

"I got a call from the cops."

"I'll be there in five minutes."

He didn't ask what it was about or anything, he just said he was on his way. That told me a lot right there. I was waiting for him when he walked in.

"You have to get your shit and get out of here."

"Carol - "

"I've been downstairs already. In the closet."

He looked a little worried then. "I can explain."

"You know what, Joe? I don't want you to explain," I said. "I just want you out of here. And take all that crap with you. All of it. They already got Skippy."

"How'd you know that?"

"Because I know. I got a call. Now get a move on."

"Carol, you're making this into a big deal."

"A big deal?" I was furious. "Skippy was arrested for drugs, Joe, not jaywalking. It's a very big deal. Jerry wouldn't have called me if it wasn't a big deal."

"That son of a bitch!"

"Hey, Jerry's not the son of a bitch, you're the son of a bitch! This is my house, Joe. You brought this shit into my house. Not your house, my house. My house, where I live with my son!"

He kind of snapped to attention when I mentioned Ryan. He knew I would do anything to protect my son.

"Now get all your shit and get out of here right now."

I went to the door to leave, but before I did, I had one more thing to say to him.

"I know people, too, Joe." Which was true. Joe may have been connected to some bad people, but I had Jerry and Mr. Constantino and a lot of other people who wouldn't appreciate the fact if he gave me any trouble.

I walked across the street to the Constantinos' house. The old man was waiting for me with Ryan.

"Everything all right?"

"Just a little trouble at home," I said.

"I heard."

Which didn't mean he heard us yelling, it meant that he already knew about Skippy and so he also knew about Joe. Word travels fast in the neighborhood.

"I'm going to take Ryan out for a hamburger."

"Good idea," the old man said. "I think I'll sit on my porch and wait."

Which meant he would be watching Joe so none of my things somehow got mixed in with his things. The old man may have slowed down a step or two, but he was a pretty sharp cookie. He was a well-respected man.

"Go," he said, "have a good time."

While we were at dinner, Joe did as he was told and moved everything out, and that was the end of our relationship. The guy that had been bugging me to marry him every couple of months for three years was out of my life forever.

Well, almost. I still had all of my salon stuff at his shop, and I needed to figure out what I was going to do. I didn't want to just close my business. I'd worked hard for it. Gone to school, built my client list.

So as uncomfortable as it was, I worked out of the shop for about another month. And business was booming. Everybody was coming in because they wanted to hear all the gossip.

Joe and I had an understanding about what we would say and what we wouldn't say, and we stuck to it. I wasn't looking to hurt him, I just wanted to be rid of him.

Eventually, I moved my facial business into my basement, which was ironic, in a way. Joe had helped me find the guy to fix the place up as a rental so I could earn some extra money, and now because of Joe I was right back in the basement, earning a little extra money.

I was very upset about the whole thing. Not only had Joe lied to me, but he had done his business in front of Ryan. Maybe while he was upstairs, but my son was in the house. He told me that he didn't, but I knew better. All those times I was out of town, Joe was alone with Ryan. I never saw him bring any of that stuff into the house when I was there, so he must have done when I was gone. When he was supposed to be looking out for my son. What if there had been a problem? These were people who carried guns and dealt drugs. What if somebody had gotten shot or killed while my son was in the house.

Even today, it makes me mad to think about it.

Ryan took our breakup pretty hard. He had been deeply affected by the divorce, and Joe was the first guy since Cody who really filled that role for him when he wasn't with his dad down in Texas. And he just really liked Joe.

But I made Joe promise not to talk to Ryan, or even be around him, and he knew I was serious. But it wasn't like Joe dropped off the face of the earth or anything. He was still around the neighborhood. He didn't get arrested. So Ryan saw him all the time, and Joe had to give him the cold shoulder, which Ryan didn't understand.

But that's the way it had to be. You put my son at risk, that's not something I can forgive. Not by a long shot.

Ryan didn't know the full story for a very long time, but when he was older I talked to him about it. Even as a kid, he understood there was a lot of bad stuff happening around Joe and his family.

Joe's nephew, who's just a few years older than Ryan's, went to prison not too long ago for attempted murder. He got kicked out of school, fell in with a gang, and repeatedly stabbed a young girl behind the car wash where he worked, a job I helped him get. He's the son of Joe's brother, the one their mother spoiled rotten, and her grandson turned out the same way. I couldn't have Ryan around that kind of thing.

Nothing like that was ever going to happen to my son. Not if I could help it.

We had our moments, though.

15

Ryan

I T GOES WITHOUT SAYING THAT EVERY PARENT IS proud of their kids. It's part of being a human being. It's in our DNA. You look in their eyes and you see possibilities. You see hope. And you see unconditional love. Every word your own parents ever spoke to you comes back and you immediately understand how they felt about you. Suddenly, you know.

When you're a mother and it's your son, you see the man you want him to become, and for better or worse, you see his father. You look into the eyes of this little person you carried around inside you for many months and you just fall in love. The entire world is reflected back to you in his bright, shiny little eyes. You hold him in your arms and there's nothing you wouldn't do for the little guy.

And you worry.

You worry about the possibilities.

Suddenly the world is an unbelievably beautiful place, and the most dangerous place you can imagine. And you start to get that parenting is a very tough job. As hard as it is, you end up wishing it were that easy.

But my son has had it tough, too. He's overcome a lot in his life.

Ryan wasn't born in the easiest of circumstances. His father was totally opposed to having a family and pretty much demanded that I end the pregnancy as soon as he found out about it. This was not a totally selfish position on his part, of course, because of my health issues. The doctors all told me the same thing; I should not have this baby.

But every reason they gave me to terminate the pregnancy, I saw a reason to have him. When they told that I wasn't supposed to get pregnant, I just saw it as proof that I was.

His father came around from the moment he held Ryan in his arms, as I knew he would, but it didn't change the man he was and it didn't change the problems in our marriage.

The divorce was tough on Ryan, as I'm sure it is for most children. The two people he loved most in the world no longer loved each other.

So he was mad. He was a great kid, but there was a lot of anger there about the divorce, about what was happening to me, how sick I got, about a lot of things. He was also diagnosed with ADD and had dyslexia, and he had a tough time in school as a result. We moved around a lot, too, so that's always hard on a kid, because you're changing schools and having to make new friends and trying to fit into new places.

Ryan used to check under the dining room table and count the different colors of tape the movers inevitably left there to keep track or how many times we moved. I hated uprooting him, but I was a single mother and I had to go where I could work.

He was a big kid, too, and a stutterer for a while, so you can imagine the problems at school. He barely even spoke until he was three years old. He just seemed to be taking his time getting started with everything, which is why I'm so amazed at the man he's become.

But his childhood was tough. He saw a therapist for several years to deal with his anger issues, and he was put into special education classes. He had tutors and went to the Sylvan Learning Center a couple of days a week after school. The school administrators told me that he'd never get out of special ed, but he worked his ass off and he did. Then they said he'd probably have to go to a trade tech high school, but he went to DePaul Catholic High School. He was even accepted to Seton Hall Prep. Ryan was always a very hard worker.

His father was not a lot of help, I'm sorry to say. When Ryan was prescribed Ritalin, I noticed an improvement in his ability to focus, which is a big part of the learning process. I know a lot of people don't like that particular medication, but it worked for my son. But when he visited his dad in the summer, Cody would tell Ryan it was bad for him and take him right off it. And of course, kids don't like to take medicine, anyway, and Ryan was no different. He was running around and playing and who needed to stop and take a pill? So that was a routine struggle with my ex-husband and that didn't help matters.

But Ryan overcame that, too.

He's also one of the most charitable young men you could ever meet. Having a mother who was sick off and on from the day he was born contributed to that, I'm sure.

When he was about ten years old, I got mugged after dark in Patterson. I was still working for the Radisson at the time, before my time at WebMD, and I had to get a lot of promotional materials printed at a copy store that was open late, worked cheap, and had a very fast turn around.

Two guys grabbed me behind the building, but I managed to get away and run screaming through this dark alley. Somebody was look-ing out for me, though, because even though it was late and I was in a completely unfamiliar area and had no idea where I was going, the first unlocked door I found turned out to be the back entrance to the offices of a rape crisis center.

I was really shaken up, and it had quite an impact on Ryan. When he found out what happened, from that moment on he insisted on going with me whenever I went places he thought were dangerous, one of which was a soup kitchen where I volunteered. He was so sweet and protective of his mother.

"Mom, you're not going there without me and that's that."

He was in the fourth grade.

And the thing is, he really liked going there. He saw all the people who were having a rough time, and he felt very badly for them. At ten years old, he was into serving food to the homeless. I was so proud of him.

That whole experience kind of kick started Ryan in his charity work, which continues to this day. It was a real eye opener for him, seeing all those kids his own age who had nothing. We struggled sometimes, but we always had a roof over our heads and a support system in place. We had family and friends and hot meals. He was really surprised and touched to see those homeless kids.

It was certainly a lot different from running around a big, fancy hotel.

Not long after that, he put together an MS walk with one of his teachers at school, which ended up raising over ten thousand dollars. Ryan got the police department involved, state troopers, the football team had a car wash, the whole town played a part. It was a very big deal for a fifth grader. I had always been a big volunteer; I even wanted to join the Peace Corps, but Ryan was amazing. A kid in middle school doing what he did, it blew me away.

He's done MS walks and bike rides every year since, and he would do things like that even if I didn't have the disease. That's just the kind of person he is.

I think back to when he was a baby, and wondering if he would grow up to be like his father, and he's grown up to be so much better. He would hate me saying that, but it's the truth. He turned out to be a wonderful man, and he'll make a fine husband and father some day.

But it's been a long, hard road, and he overcame a lot.

Brain surgery, for example.

If all of our troubles weren't enough, just before Joe and I broke up, Ryan started getting these terrible headaches. Awful migraines. It was so painful to see him like that; you could literally see his veins popping out of his head.

I took him to all kinds of doctors, but nobody could tell me what was wrong with him, which made me crazy. There's something wrong with your kid, and they can't put a name on it. Just tell me what it is and I can fight it. They would prescribe medications, but nothing was helping. He'd wake up in the middle of the night screaming.

It was bad.

Finally one of the doctors told me that I needed to take him to NYU.

"There's something really wrong here, but it's beyond me," he said.

Even though that was a scary thing to hear, I appreciated him telling me that. Doctors can be arrogant sometimes. When they don't know something, they don't always want to admit it. Sometimes they'd rather just prescribe something different to see if it works, but this guy just flat out admitted that he was in over his head with Ryan. He was the first doctor to tell us that.

We went to NYU.

Our doctor was really young; my first thought was that he looked like a baby, Doogie Howser or something. He ordered a CAT scan, which had been done numerous times before, and an MRI, which had also been done several times. Nothing had ever been found by any of those doctors.

Doogie found something.

There was a blood abscess in Ryan's brain. An aneurysm. Like a little balloon of blood in his artery. It was congenital; apparently a lot of young men have them and never even know unless they have a problem, like Ryan's headaches. There's no way to know you have it without imaging the brain, and what young person has that done?

So whenever you hear about a young man suddenly dropping dead for no reason, this is sometimes the cause.

We were very lucky. Ryan's headaches were a blessing in disguise, because they alerted us to the problem. I was so happy we finally knew what was wrong, but I nearly fainted when the doctor told me what they would have to do.

For Ryan's brain surgery, to get where they needed to go to take care of the abscess, they had to literally take his ear off and drill into his skull, drain the abscess or whatever it is that they do, and then sew his ear back on. It would affect his hearing in that ear, of course, but that was the least of our worries. At least they didn't have to do a craniotomy. Perspective is everything.

The operation took seven hours, and I was a basket case the whole time, of course. I was a mess from the time we got the diagnosis, actually. It was a very scary time. I was also had to deal with Cody.

His father refused to come in town for the surgery, which really pissed me off.

"That's not what I do," he said. "That's what you do."

That's not what you do? You're his father!

My entire family was there, my parents, brother and sisters, Joe, friends of mine, practically everyone I knew, and the first person Ryan asked for when he woke up?

His father. It broke my heart. My boy had been through so much, and his dad didn't even bother to come in for his surgery. I wanted to kill him.

Ryan loves his dad and they have a very good relationship, but he was very upset about that, I could tell, as well he should have been. But since he was just a kid, he made excuses for his father at first, like children do.

He was busy drilling oil, I'll see him in the summer, that kind of thing. I let Ryan believe what he wanted to believe. All I was concerned about was getting my son better, and I've never been one of those people to use her child to score points against the other side. Eventually Ryan figured things out on his own and has come to terms with who his father is, and he accepts him and loves him. And that makes me happy.

Ryan missed about six months of the eighth grade because a thing like that takes a long time to heal, and going to school was just too dangerous. If he'd gotten hit in the head or something, he could have done serious damage.

The teacher the school sent over didn't know what she was doing, so I hired a kid from the local high school, Steven Diamato, to tutor Ryan, and he turned out to be a great choice. He was really smart and absolutely thrilled to get paid eleven bucks an hour to hang out with Ryan and show him all the stuff he'd already learned.

They did homework together, played video games, even a little basketball once Ryan was up to it. He was like a big brother to him.

Steven was a good role model, too; honor roll, captain of the football team, he went to our church. I couldn't have found anyone better for the job. He and Ryan got along great, and over time became really good friends.

Ryan's surgery and recovery was a very big milestone in our lives. It was pivotal because things could have turned out so much differently than they did. Besides the fact that the surgery itself could have gone badly and didn't, there were a lot of other things that could have gone wrong.

He could have held onto the anger against his father for not being there, but Ryan forgave him. He could have fallen behind in school, but he worked really hard and didn't. He could have reacted badly when he had to quit basketball; he could have turned to drugs or alcohol or the wrong crowd of kids, but he didn't do any of those things.

Ryan could have turned out like Joe's nephew, but he didn't. He was grateful that he was alive; every day after that was a gift to Ryan. He could have gone in so many other directions after all that had happened, but he didn't. He truly developed a love for life that has kept him on the right path to this day.

He didn't rebel against me, or his father, or society. He didn't run away from his problems, or make excuses for them, or look for answers in all the wrong places.

Ryan worked through them. He overcame them. He beat them. He's a fighter, just like his mother.

My son is one of the strongest men I know.

16

Perfect Match

RYAN AND I WERE BETTER OFF GETTING AWAY from Joe and his criminal enterprises, but the breakup was pretty tough on both of us, if I'm being honest. Even though I was furious with him for allowing my son to be around all of that, we had been together for a few years and it was hard. He was a father figure for Ryan, and that was hard, too. A single mother with a son is always looking for role models.

The money was tough. I had to dip into the settlement from WebMD more than I wanted to because I was not making as much money. I found another shop to do my facials, but now I had to pay out for the space. When you're on disability, they only allow you to work so much before they cut you off, anyway, and I needed the health benefits that came with it.

To tell you the truth, I couldn't have worked as much anyway because I was tired all the time. It was like I had crossed a line and the disease decided to take a greater hold on my life. The words of the doctors were really starting to sink in. I was not going to be able to work again, not like I had before. I understood intellectually that that was the case, but I was beginning to understand in my heart and soul, and it was hard for me to deal with. I even had to use a cane periodically, which felt strange and just added to my depression, and being depressed just makes the MS worse.

A lot of my former customers for the facials stopped coming in because they wanted to be loyal to Joe, so it was a weird situation. Eventually I stopped doing facials altogether because it just made me too fatigued.

I also lost the regular PR work I had been doing for this local businessman for years because he was the owner of the car wash where I'd gotten Joe's nephew a job, which was where he'd stabbed that girl. It wasn't my fault, of course, but the owner hated all of the bad publicity and it soured our business relationship. I'm not sure I had the energy, anyway. I still did the events for the sheriff's department for free, but I slowed down quite a bit.

The saving grace in all of this was that I was still repping the MS drugs. Bayer had bought out Berlex labs by that point, but they didn't get rid of anybody, thank God. And they were very understanding of my situation, because who better to understand MS than the company who treated the disease?

So I gave talks and trained their reps, and they still flew me around the country, sometimes with Ryan. They were good about that. It was a blessing.

It helped with my depression, too. I met a lot of great people at those events, people I'm still friends with to this day. Generally speaking, I had a good social life.

But I was lonely. I wanted to settle down. I've never really been someone who wanted to date a lot of guys. I wanted to make a home with someone, find a decent guy to be a stepfather to my son, someone he could look up to.

I'd always had men, as my mother would say, "sniffing around," but there was no one who was really up to Ryan's standards, or my own.

I tried Internet dating sites, and that was hit or miss, as you can imagine. There was one guy I brought home, but Ryan hated him, so that was the end of that. Most I didn't even think of introducing to my son. One guy posted a picture of himself that looked like a Latin lover, and then when I met him, he was Black. That didn't bother me, but I had to ask him about the picture because there was just no resemblance.

"What, are you racist?" He asked.

"No, are you a liar?" I answered.

There was no second date.

I met a guy who seemed nice, but turned out to be an alcoholic. Another guy was married. It was your typical assemblage of random men, a lot of whom just weren't good enough for my son.

I started meeting them all at the same Italian restaurant where I was friends with the owners, so if there was any trouble, my date would be made to leave. All I had to do was give a nod to the bar. It became almost like a series of job interviews. As soon as the guy sat down, I could pretty much tell if it was going to work. But I ate a lot of free linguine.

Then I met Mark.

His profile was different than a lot of guys. He was very direct and open, very honest. Some profiles you can just tell. He didn't seem to be bragging like a lot of men, he was just providing information. After my past experiences, that was greatly appreciated, believe me.

He was a widower, which was fit with what I was looking for. He had been married before, so it wasn't his first rodeo. His wife had passed from breast cancer, and he had taken care of her, which impressed me. Widowed or divorced was okay, married or separated was not. I wasn't interested in a man with young children, which he wasn't. Grown children, I could take, but little kids would be too hard. He was financially independent, which was a plus, of course. There are a lot of guys out there who were looking to be taken care of, believe me. He'd been with the same company for almost thirty years.

He was also Italian, which was good, but he wasn't in the Mafia, which would have been bad. As a matter of fact, Mark was like the anti-Mafia. Not a crime fighter, just the least Mafia-like guy you could imagine. He was very conservative, not a rule breaker or a risk taker at all, which was good, because I was. Not big risks. Little ones. For example, I was a speeder and he wasn't. That type of thing. He even came to a complete stop at stop signs.

In other words, he was the yin to my yang. We complimented each other very well. He was a very calm, whereas I can be a little hyper sometimes. So it seemed like a good match. We talked on the phone for a long time before we finally went out on an actual date. My sister had just adopted an adorable baby girl, but she was sick a lot and I broke a lot of dates to go take care of her or babysit, and Mark was always a gentleman about it. He never questioned me, he just accepted it and waited until I was free.

Just an all around good guy.

And then we went out, and I discovered the truth.

He wasn't a good guy. He was a great guy. All of those long phone conversations we shared before we actually met, getting to know each other more slowly that we might otherwise have, were prelude to something really wonderful.

I told him all about my health issues that night. I practically gave him my medical records. I never wanted to keep any of that from anyone because it affected my life in every way, but especially Mark. Mark was a keeper, I could tell that, and I wanted to lay everything out on the table.

None of that mattered to Mark.

He told me everything, too. All about his wife, who had died only six months before. How he took care of her. I could definitely relate. Mark was a caregiver. That was just the kind of man he was. His mother also died from breast cancer very young, so he shared my passion for patients' rights and other medical issues.

It was a Match.com made in heaven.

We were both from northern New Jersey, brought up Catholic, from middle class backgrounds, although I considered my family poor compared to his. He had a stay-at-home mom who baked every day, a father who wore a suit to work, his family took annual vacations, and they had a new car every two or three years.

To me, that was rich!

Just a mom who baked her own bread was like something out of a science fiction movie compared to how I had grown up. Milk and cake every night? Fuggedaboutit!

He was very sweet and more than a little nervous, which I found endearing. And his obvious compassion was very attractive to me. He treated the wait staff very nicely, which is always a good sign. If I went on a date with a man who treated others like servants, how was he going to treat me? So it was all good. We got along great from the very first date, with one exception.

"I have to tell you," I said, "I never want to get married again."

He didn't look thrilled with that, but he didn't duck the issue.

"Well, I'm the marrying kind of guy," he answered. "I don't think I could just live with someone."

"How do you know? You married your wife right out of high school."

He had to admit I had a point. But I could see in his eyes that he wasn't convinced. Mark wanted to be married. It was obvious. But he seemed to be keeping his options open because he really liked me. I could tell that, too.

He hugged me at the end of the date, and that was all. He didn't try to kiss me, which was very gentlemanly, of course. And we went our separate ways.

He emailed me when he got home, but I didn't check my computer, and when he called the next morning I was on a short hike on Garret Mountain, so it went to voicemail. When I got back to my car, I finally checked my phone and called him back.

He called to see if I wanted to go for a hike in the mountains.

We laughed, and decided to go for another hike. I went home and made myself a little more presentable and met him at the same trailhead and showed him this very nice spot overlooking West Paterson, and then we went back down the mountain and he took me to lunch.

We got lost in conversation, and by the time we left it was getting dark and had started to snow. By the time we got back to Garret Mountain, they had closed the gates with my car in there.

I was just going to walk around the gates and drive back out, but he wouldn't let me do that because it was so cold. So he drove me past all of these signs that said keep out and park closed, which was probably the first time he'd ever broken the law in his life. He was very cute.

It meant something to me that he did that because I knew he was such a boy scout. There was no way he wasn't going to stay with me every minute to make sure I was safe and warm. It was very important to him, and that made it very romantic to me.

He followed me home since it was really coming down, and took me inside but absolutely refused to stay the night, even on the couch, because that's what it would have been, anyway, since Ryan was in the house.

Ryan grilled him, too. I had already told him about Mark and showed him his profile picture and all that, so Ryan was ready.

Where do you work, how much do you make, how many kids do you have?

I swear, Ryan was worse than my father.

Mark answered every question.

I had been worried about Ryan because it had been just him and me for a while. He had been the man of the house, and so I thought he might feel threatened if I got serious about anyone. There hadn't been anyone steady since Joe, and Ryan was just kind of getting over that.

I told Mark all of that, and he wasn't worried.

"I think this is meant to be."

It was our second date. February 11, 2007.

"I feel really good with you, Mark," I said. "And I trust you. But that's all I can give you right now."

It took him three hours to get home that night because of the storm, and the next day we drove out to Paterson Falls to see the frozen water and the snow and it was all so pristine and beautiful. There was this photographer taking pictures for the newspaper, and he just assumed we were together and took our picture, which Mark still has.

When he took me home, he started talking about how this would be his first Valentine's Day without a someone, and this went on for several minutes, and for some reason it went right over my head that he was asking me out. Finally he got through to me by just coming out with it, already.

"I want to take you out for Valentine's Day."

I looked deeply into my future husband's beautiful brown eyes and said,

"No."

I quickly explained that it wasn't that I didn't want to go out with him, but that being in the hotel business for all those years made me hate going out on the actual day, with the reservations and the crowds and all of that.

"Why don't I cook for us?"

He really liked that idea, too.

We decided to cook at his house, though. It was a forty-five minute drive each way, but he insisted on picking me up and taking me home after. His sons Mathew and Christopher were grown and out of the house and it was a school night, so it seemed like the more romantic way to go about the most romantic day of the year.

We went shopping for groceries, and he had such a good time doing that. He liked the normality of it, and he liked being with me. Simple pleasures. He was growing on me by the minute.

I did have to educate him on the finer cuts of meat, however. He was a pretty frugal guy, but being in the hospitality business, I knew the place to go for a good steak was a butcher shop, always. He was amazed that meat could cost that much, but he was game. It was whole new world of food for him.

He wasn't a rube or anything, though. He was one of the few guys on Match.com who knew what my screen name meant, which was Cakebread96. You can imagine what some guys thought. I was a baker or a cupcake or something. But Mark recognized it as a wine right away, which was another thing that impressed me. The '96 Cabernet sauvignon was fantastic, and a man who recognized that was a man after my own heart.

That screen name was like a filter; it really cut down on the riff-raff.

He also asked his sons for advice on what to get me for a gift, and mentioned that to me ion the phone the night before our big night, which was pretty shrewd, as well. He was basically letting me know that he had gotten me something so I wouldn't feel bad. He was very good with the little things that make a big difference. A very considerate man.

So I got him some really nice chocolates, and he gave me two bottles of Cakebread '96 and a dozen roses. It was lovely.

He did everything right.

It was just about the best Valentine's Day this girl had ever had, and a great way to end our very first week together.

We've been together ever since.

I guess I was the marrying kind, after all.

17

Inlaws and Outlaws

WHAT REALLY CLINCHED IT FOR ME WAS how Mark was with my crazy family. I knew I was in love for sure the following Christmas, when I brought Mark over to my sister Joanne's house with his sons in tow and instructions to my relatives to please keep the cursing and general insanity to a minimum.

Very few men I dated ever made it that far. Meeting all my relatives was just too intense of an experience for most human beings to handle. But Mark and I had been dating for almost a year, we'd gone a beautiful cruise together for ten days, and you really get to know someone on a cruise. Trust me, those cabins are tiny. So it had to happen sometime. Eventually, he was going to meet my family.

I said a prayer and threw the poor guy to the wolves.

There were members of my family who had already met Mark, of course. I wasn't keeping him a secret, or anything. It's just that my family is much better in small doses. You meet my mother here, my sister there, that kind of thing.

But all together? At Christmas? That was very dangerous. Holidays in my family are big, rowdy affairs. Actually, forget holidays. Anytime my family is all in one place, for whatever reason, bring bail money.

Everyone drinks and argues and curses and yells and generally has the time of their lives. It's not for the faint of heart, believe me.

My sister Joanne had actually seen Mark's profile on Match.com before I did, and told me if I fucked this one up, she was going to kill me because Mark was definitely a keeper.

"I mean it," she said. "This guy is really good, so if you're not serious, let him go. He's not like us, he's decent!"

I had to laugh at that, but I knew what she meant. Our whole family was nuts, and Mark was a normal guy by comparison.

"There are plenty of women out there looking for a decent guy, Carol. Don't ruin someone else's chance."

"All right, I get it," I said, and I did.

My sister considered me fickle when it came to men, which I suppose I was. I mean, I'm a good person and all, but when it came to men, they were kind of disposable. I could take them or leave them. I always seemed to have one around when I needed him, and not when I didn't.

But even I got that Mark wasn't that kind of guy. While I wanted to move slowly before I committed, I knew that if I moved too slowly, he would find somebody else. He was a man among men.

So I prepared Mark as best I could. "My family's just not like yours," I warned him. "You had a mother who stayed home and baked bread and a father who went to work in a suit, your brothers all played sports and got along. That's not my family. My parents are divorced, everybody drinks too much, half of them are Democrats and the other half are Republicans and all of them are too damn loud about it, and - "

"Carol, I get it," he laughed.

I actually said a prayer that he would be laughing after the party.

He was.

We went to Christmas dinner, which was a great big Italian bacchanal. Basically a Roman orgy without the sex, although knowing some of my nephews and cousins, I wouldn't completely rule that out.

And Mark was great. Perfect. He and his sons made it through unscathed. Joanne helped a lot to do with that, actually. She's always been, and it was her house. She didn't take crap from anyone, and she read everybody the riot act ahead of time.

"You're all gonna behave yourselves. This is a nice guy for Carol. No getting drunk, no smoking pot, no beating the crap out of each other, none of that shit is happening! Understood?"

And everybody was pretty good. I was surprised.

Of course, no one can actually get my mother to behave, but I watched how Mark handled her abruptness. She could be downright rude sometimes, but he dealt with her in such a kind, patient way, he actually made her nicer!

He had that effect on my whole family. He kind of made them all nice just because he was so sweet and gentle. It was amazing. Everybody really wanted to get to know him, and it went great. As I watched him with my family, he was like the eye of the hurricane, the calm in the center of the storm.

Mark was the Cetrino whisperer.

I fell in love with him that day. Whatever doubts I had melted away. He was so wonderful with the children, especially my niece. I could tell he was a wonderful father, great with both my son and my dad, very respectful to everyone. Just a really good man.

He even went to church with me, which he didn't really like, but he did it for me. A guy who'll sit through a long church service when he really doesn't want to be there is a special guy. He'd kind of forgotten when to kneel and what to say, but it was effort that impressed me.

Mark told me that he loved me a few weeks after we met, but I had not been ready to say that before that Christmas. I could only bring myself to answer, "I really care for you," which is not at all what someone wants to hear when they put themselves out there like that. Mark was patient, though, and after seeing him with my family, I had no reservations at all.

I had found my guy.

The first time I actually said the words was at our favorite restaurant, after Christmas and before New Year's.

"I love you, you know."

"You do?" He asked, like he knew it was coming but he couldn't believe he'd finally heard it. It was a long time coming, and he was really happy.

"I do. I really do."

When I look back, though, I knew he was the one from our very first date. We both did. It just took a while for me to say the words.

We started to talk about things, make plans like couples do. I told him that when my son graduated high school the following spring, I wanted to leave New Jersey. I was ready for a change. I'd been all over the country, seen some really nice places, and I figured a warmer climate was where I wanted to be.

"Maybe Mesa, Arizona," I told him, "or Atlanta."

"My company has an office in Atlanta," he answered. "We have ties to Mesa, too. Maybe it's time for a fresh start."

That was a very good answer.

For Ryan's graduation, we had a big party, and I couldn't invite Mark because of Cody. I was so pissed off. Cody, who wouldn't travel to his son's bedside for his brain surgery, who had never once left Texas to visit his son after we left the state, suddenly decided he was coming to the high school graduation party.

I had to allow it; it was Ryan's dad. But it would have been a disaster if the two of them had been there. It ended up being kind of a disaster, anyway, but I just couldn't trust Cody at that point. It was just too tense. Ryan felt the same way. Cody was like a wild person in those days, and nobody knew what he would do. I didn't know what my own family would do, either, to tell you the truth. They were pretty crazy.

I was glad that he brought Ryan's grandparents, Gus and Edith, though. Gus passed away about six months later, so it was nice that he got to see his grandson graduate, and nice that Ryan got to see him before he died.

Mark was very mature about it. He understood completely, and even made all the centerpieces for the tables at Bellisimo's, which was my favorite restaurant and where we'd gone on our first date and where I first told him I loved him. We went there all the time. Mark was very creative and good with crafts, and they looked fantastic.

I know he was a little hurt, but he didn't complained. He loved my family and he loved Ryan, and so he would have loved to have gone to the party. To be honest, even after Cody said he was coming, I would not have been at all surprised if he changed his mind at the last minute, but in the end I'm glad he showed up. Ryan would have been so disappointed if his father had backed out after the shock of actually confirming his attendance.

I knew for sure that Gus and Edith would be there because I made all their travel arrangements. I even paid for their tickets and hotel, which was a little strange. Edith asked me to take care of all their reservations, which I did, and I just assumed they would make arrangements to pay me. It never happened. They had money, so I have no idea why. They were simple people, so maybe they just assumed that was how it worked, like the father of the bride paying for the guests or something.

I had planned a beautiful party for about thirty-five people after the actual graduation ceremony, very elegant, with a smaller gathering the night before at Joanne's house so the family could all get reacquainted. Gus and Edith were there and it was very nice and low key. So far, so good.

The next night was when all hell broke loose.

After the graduation ceremony, Gus had a terrible allergic reaction to something, and Cody was going to take his mother and father back to their hotel, rest a bit, and then bring his mom back to the party.

Two hours later, he still hadn't shown up because he got lost.

The hotel was ten minutes away.

Ryan actually had to leave his own party with his cousin Mickey to go and get them. Granted, it was spaghetti junction around there with all the intersecting highways, but two hours?

Take a cab, you idiot!

By this time everybody had had their appetizers and they're all getting smashed, and it was really screwing up the kitchen, holding the dinner that long. So even though I was only serving beer and wine because I thought that would keep my family sober a little longer than if they had vodka and whiskey, everyone was good and drunk by the time Ryan and his dad got back.

For all I know, my family brought flasks.

My sister Barbara was out of control, one of my nephews was drunk out of his mind and put out a cigarette in the palm of Ryan's hand, a scar that he still has; it was a nightmare. My oldest sister Janet, the mother of the miscreant kid with the cigarette who has since reformed himself, thank God, would have never let her son do that if she had been there, but she was off somewhere getting an award from The Mental Health Association of New Jersey, which was ironic, to say the least.

It got really crazy after that.

People were breaking glasses in the parking lot; my father was screaming at people to quiet down, it was a regular melee.

Typical Cetrino family outing.

After all that, Cody turned out to be the least of my worries.

I actually had not even seen him since Ryan was in the sixth grade when I had business in Dallas and he drove up to pick him up at DFW Airport.

Our reunion was a little cold and perfunctory, but he didn't cause me any problems. It was tolerable. He did look very uncomfortable because he had to get dressed up, at least 'dressed up' for Cody.

He was wearing the exact same outfit he wore when we got married. I couldn't believe it. Boots, khaki pants, white shirt, blue blazer. The same ugly striped tie. Twelve years later, it was all the same.

Every single day I thank the good Lord I met Mark.

Edith was very straitlaced, and she didn't know what to make of all the goings-on. She was also a little preoccupied thinking of her ailing husband back at the hotel, and so after the cake was served, Ryan took her back to the hotel.

My son, at his own graduation, was shuttling everybody back and forth. That's Ryan. I told him I could call her a cab, but he said it was his dad's mom and he wanted to help her. What a great kid.

I thought about making Cody drive her back, but we'd probably never see either one of them again.

Was I ever ready to get out of Dodge!

18

Empty Nest, Itchy Feet

CRIED FOR WEEKS WHEN RYAN LEFT FOR COLLEGE. I
knew it was coming for a long time, of course, but that didn't make
it any easier. It's what every parent dreads. You raise your kid the
best you can, and when they get to a certain age, everything they
do either makes you so proud you cry or makes you so angry you cry
some more. Or they make you laugh until you cry or cry until you
can't. Whichever it was for me, there was a lot of crying involved.

And you never want to let them go, even though you know you
have to. Everything you've done for them their entire life has been
leading to the moment they leave the nest, and then you realize you'd
give anything to just hold them close for a little longer.

But then you remember how it was for you at that age, and you
understand why you have to let them go.

For better or worse, Ryan was leaving home to make his way in
the world, and for better or worse, I was completely beside myself.

Even though I had incredible confidence in the young man he had
become, it was still very frightening for me. He was at the age when

things happen. Things that I couldn't control. Of course, there are always a lot of things beyond the control of a parent, but when children are young, at least you can exercise your authority. Seeing Ryan as a young man made me realize just how little control I actually had. So I learned all over again how to leave everything in God's hands. What was around the corner would just have to be dealt with at the time.

People with MS usually learn this pretty quickly. Our disease can be very fickle. You learn to expect the unexpected. One moment you're fine and the next you're completely disabled. One moment you're walking through a shopping mall listening to Christmas music, and the next you're in the hospital because you suddenly went blind.

MS is like the mystery and uncertainty of life times ten; you never know what's going to happen, and the chances are always better than even that things can turn pretty bad, pretty quickly.

Ryan was just as aware of this as I was, by the way. He'd been living with the knowledge that his mother could die at any time since he was six years old. He knew all about MS from a very early age because I was always as honest and open with him as I could be about my health. It was important that I prepared him for my death. It sounds awful, I know, but it was necessary. As a result, MS has been as much a part of his life as it has been of mine.

That's one of the amazing things about my son, how he's dealt with my disease. It's ironic that all of my doctors used MS as the primary reason not to have Ryan, but he turned out to be the one person without whom I could not have survived it.

Living with an incurable disease means you prepare. There are advances in treatment and new drugs, but MS does not get better. That's not so say I've given up on a cure because I haven't. But I know

I may not see it. So you live your life and you try not to dwell on the inevitable, but it's always there in the back of your mind. It follows you like a malevolent shadow, and every now and then the disease rears its ugly head to remind you how fragile life really is.

It's very easy to get depressed, and I've had my share of those dark days. But MS has also taught me a great deal. Every breath, every moment, every day is a blessing. Good days and bad days, they are all to be treasured in their own particular way.

Ryan had been with me every step of the way as I lived with MS, which made things a lot easier for me. Which just meant it was even harder when it was time to let him go. I was very blessed that Mark came into my life when he did, I really was.

However, I still had to come to terms with the fact that Ryan would no longer be right there beside me so that I could protect him, and he would no longer be right there to protect me. It was the end of a long journey for both of us, and for both of us, a new beginning.

Even so, as difficult as the road had been, I would not have changed a thing.

Everything happens for a reason; whether we understand it at the time or not, and we are all part of God's infinite design. I don't believe in accidents. Each of us has freedom of choice, but there is also a plan for our lives. There is a path God has laid out for us, and it's our job to follow it as best we can. Everything has a reason.

For example, when I found out I had MS, I made the choice to stop doing drugs and to straighten out my life.

A big part of that was focusing on work. As a result, I became very good at sales, and if I hadn't developed that particular skill, I wouldn't have known how to hook up with all of those doctors and drug companies and been able to tell my story to so many people, and thus do my part to influence their lives for the better.

Had I not been diagnosed with MS, I would not have had all of the experience with medical issues and doctors and treatments, and so I would not have known to get Ryan an MRI.

Without the MRI, we would never have discovered the aneurysm in his brain, and my son would have died like so many otherwise healthy young men who have no idea there's anything wrong until their aneurysm ruptures. Most people don't understand all the intricacies of our health insurance system, and how much education matters when we get sick. Just learning how to navigate the system can mean the difference between life and death, and the knowledge I acquired because of my disease saved the life of my son.

All of those things didn't just happen; they were part of God's will. His plan for my life. God has a plan for all of us, I'm certainly not special or anything. Whether we choose to accept it or not is what makes the difference in our lives. I've tried to use my experiences to help others with MS, and I've accepted the disease as part of His plan. If nothing else, MS has taught me the power of acceptance.

Of course, accepting hardship for my son was another story.

Looking back over my life, it still amazes me how many times I nearly lost him. When he was a newborn I thought I was going to lose him with that crazy illness no one ever really figured out. When he had brain surgery as an adolescent, I thought I might lose him. And when his father bought him that stupid Firebird for his senior year in high school…well, that one may have been the hardest to accept because it was so easily avoidable.

It began with yet another dispute with Cody, who gave Ryan the money for the car against my wishes. We really fought about that one. Ryan was at that rebellious age, and he wanted to do what the other kids were doing. Which was drinking and driving their cars like crazy people. He had always been hyper anyway, and I really didn't want him behind the wheel of any car, let alone a Firebird. I remembered how my friends and I acted back in high school, and I didn't want to tempt fate.

I lost the argument.

Ryan got his car to start his senior year in high school, but it only lasted for a few months. He got into all kinds of trouble with the drinking and acting out, and by October I put my foot down and donated the thing to a battered woman's shelter. Ryan couldn't pay for the insurance and I'd caught him being reckless one too many times, so that was it for me.

My son had other ideas.

On Halloween night, he begged and pleaded with my sister Joanne to loan him her Mercedes. He told her he had a hot date and would be super careful, neither of which turned out to be true, and he very nearly died because of it.

He went out driving around with a buddy from school, lost control and drove into a ditch, rolling the car several times in the process. Neither one of the boys was seriously hurt, but Ryan was arrested for reckless driving and speeding.

I got the call no parent ever wants to receive, and rushed to the police station, where I found my son with only a sore wrist and a very frightened look in his eyes.

He was about to find out what scary really was.

The cops literally had to separate the two of us. Ryan is much bigger than me, but when I grabbed him by the collar and threw him up against the wall, it took the police sergeant and two of his officers to pull me off him. Ryan wanted to stay in jail after that, and I don't blame him. Neither of us said a word on the way home.

This is typical parent behavior, of course. You thank God for sparing your child and then you want to kill them yourself to teach them a lesson.

I'd seen a lot of scary things in my life, but the single most terrifying sight of all was when I looked at his car the day after his accident. It was more pancake than motor vehicle. I couldn't believe he and his friend had walked away from that. What was worse was that if they'd been in the Firebird, they wouldn't have.

That was a scary thought.

The incident seemed to wake Ryan up, and he was a pretty good kid the rest of his senior year, during which I drove him to school every day, which was not fun for either of us. Every ride was a reminder of what had happened. I was appreciative of his behavior, but that was a hell of a way to get there. I had a few choice words for my sister, too, but I know she felt almost as terrible as I did.

A few months later I met Mark, which I really needed, and not long after that I put my house on the market and got through Ryan's graduation party.

It had been a very tumultuous year, to say the least, and more big changes were on the way.

I decided I would move to Atlanta over Arizona. I had friends in both places, but the medical facilities in Atlanta were world class, and

Brenda, one of my very best friends, had been living down there for a couple of years at that point.

It took about seven months to sell my house in New Jersey, which would have been quicker except that I wasn't negotiable on the price like I probably should have been. This was 2008 and the housing market had not bottomed out yet, so I was actually pretty lucky in that regard. But it took me a while to find a place I liked in Atlanta. Fortunately, Mark was able to transfer down, and he helped me look for a house, and looked for himself, too. That poor realtor. Mark went to see seventy-six properties in three months. My husband is a very thorough man.

It was a big move for him, though. He had grown up in New Jersey and lived there his entire life. He lived with his parents, got married, and then bought a house two blocks away. He made that house a home, raised his sons there, nursed his wife through her cancer there, invested a lot of blood, sweat, and tears there. He had made a lifetime of memories in that house, the good and the bad, and it was really all he had ever known.

Ultimately, he decided a fresh start would do him some good. But it was a very big deal for him, I knew. As for me, I was used to moving around, never really settling in. Mark was the definition of settled. But he moved for a change, and he moved for love, and he moved for me, and I'm forever grateful that he did.

As always, there would be bumps along the road, however.

Ryan had enrolled at college down in Texas and seemed to make the transition very well, so at least that was a load off my mind. He's a pretty fearless kid, all things considered, and while Cody and I may not have gotten along all that well, knowing he was close to his father was a relief. Although "close" in Texas is a relative term, I suppose. It's a very big state. But I knew Cody would look after him. He really loves his son.

Mark and I were getting along very well, getting to know each other more and more. I met his father, who was a very sweet man, and we liked each other right off, which was important because Mark was very close with his dad. Both men had lost their wives to cancer at a young age, so they had a special relationship. I even bonded with his wife's sister, who turned out to be a lot like I was twenty-five years before; she loved to smoke and drink and party. It felt a little weird at first, since I was basically taking the place of her sister, but she was great about the whole thing.

"Carol," she said, "Mark took good care of my sister. Lori was sick for five years, and he did everything for her. This is his time, and he deserves to be happy. And I know you make him happy because all he does is talk about you."

That made me feel pretty good.

So I was going back and forth between New Jersey and Atlanta, staying at Mark's place while I was there. He was looking for something to buy, too, but for him it was more complicated because he had a very large house in New Jersey that he'd owned for a long time and needed to do what the IRS calls a 1031 Exchange, basically trade up, otherwise he'd get killed on capital gains.

Mark would also watch Joey for me, my sweet pit bull rescue, even though that dog scared him half to death. Joey had been the runt of the litter, and apparently some kids had done all kinds of terrible things to him before I adopted him. Joey was a wonderful dog, but to a cat person, as Mark was, a pit bull can be a little scary.

The first time he met Joey, the dog barked at him coming down the steps as Mark came in the door, and he backed right outside and fell backwards off the porch like a someone hit the reverse button on a DVD.

Ryan, who loved Joey from the moment he saw him at the shelter, laughed his head off at that. It was an auspicious beginning, but Mark eventually would take such wonderful care of Joey when he got sick, that it was truly amazing. As I said, Mark is a caregiver by nature. But for a long time, Joey would sit on Mark's foot whenever he sat down on my couch. It was Joey's adorable but semi-threatening way of protecting me.

Smart dog.

Eventually I found a place to buy, Mark found a place to buy, and we both settled into our new lives down in Atlanta, moving closer to sharing our lives together. Moving closer to where we both wanted to be.

But as always, there were a few bumps along the way.

19

Touch and Go

FOUND A NICE LITTLE TOWNHOUSE IN A NORTHERN suburb of Atlanta called Roswell, which was perfect for me. It was in a lovely area, lots of nature, and I was incredibly relieved to finally have a place to call home. It took a while, though.

Mark encouraged me to take my time, because as an insurance guy and someone who knew how things were built, he knew all of the little things to look for when buying a house. He was constantly warning me off this place or that because of various problems most people might not concern themselves with. It was like going home shopping with a building inspector. But he was looking out for me, which was very sweet.

He was much worse when he was looking for his house, though, as I mentioned. I felt so sorry for his realtor because Mark was never satisfied. She really earned her commission when he finally bought a place.

Roswell is a beautiful city, with a lot of older homes and buildings that escaped the burning of Atlanta during the Civil War, and I just loved it right away. Lots of charm and character. I felt at peace there.

Mark found a house to buy about four months later, which was another milestone for both of us, and a relief, as well. We still weren't quite to the point of marriage and moving in together.

My neighbors to one side were an older couple from Shanghai who didn't speak much English, but they absolutely loved Mark. He would always fix little things around their house for them when he came by to see me, like a screen door that wouldn't close or a broken doorbell, and so they constantly made food for us, which was a real treat. That Mrs. Chin could really cook, let me tell you.

There was also a neighbor boy across the street named Jaimon, who was in the eighth grade and an absolute sweetheart. The nicest, most polite kid I think I ever met. The first time I met him I was walking Joey, who was sick even then, and Jaimon came right up to me and told me if I ever needed anything, to let him know.

He was Indian, and his parents were very strict and traditional, and his sister was away at college, so I think he really wanted someone to talk to. I was worn out from the move, and my poor dog, Joey was getting sick around that time, so Jaimon walked Joey for me, and we became friends. He never let me pay him, either.

He went to school and worked part-time at a nearby Wal-Mart, where his parents also worked. They were very hard working people, but had very little. When their daughter left for school they gave her their car but couldn't afford another one, so they didn't even have transportation. I think some relatives helped them buy their condo, actually.

When Wal-Mart cut Jaimon's hours, I insisted he come work for me. I was working more with HomeStretch, a non-profit group that provides support for at risk families, and there was always something I could use help with. Plus, my friend Brenda was just beginning her tragic decent into alcoholism and worse, so Jaimon would help me with her, too. If she showed up loaded and had to be taken home or to the hospital or just put to bed, Jaimon would always be available to help with "Miss Brenda", as he called her. He still calls me Miss Carol, actually. Brenda was almost like another job back then, actually, and Jaimon was a very big help.

One of my other neighbors was a single mother with three children, one of whom was autistic, and I got her to hire Jaimon to help with her kids after school. I told her there was no one I trusted more than Jaimon. He still helps her out to this day, even though he's in college. Very smart, too. He ended up getting a full academic scholarship to Georgia Tech in biomedical engineering. Jaimon is a great kid, and he's still a big part of my life.

Later on when I had to put Joey down, Jaimon was there for me. He took care of Joey when he was sick, and Jaimon didn't even like dogs. That's the kind of friend he was to me. And I needed a friend.

When Ryan first left for college, I was really busy, what with selling the house, the big move, looking for a place in Atlanta, and all the rest of it. But once I got settled in, I really missed my son. It had been just Ryan and me ever since I carried him out into the cold winter night after that horrible fight with Cody, and so being separated from my son was devastating. I was beside myself, and Jaimon helped fill the void.

It was kind of funny, because even Jaimon didn't quite get the attachment at first, and his parents certainly didn't understand it until they got to know me better. But when Ryan came to visit, he got it immediately.

"Look," he said to Jaimon, "my mom misses me. "You're nice to her, you're nice to Joey, and she needs that."

My son is a pretty smart kid, too.

They became friends and hung out every day when Ryan came to visit, which was great, and they're still friends today.

So that was my life for a while. I was working with disadvantaged families, taking care of both Joey and Brenda, and getting back to a normal, busy life. I was friends with my neighbors, and involved with their lives, as well.

Which kind of made Mark feel left out.

As I said, Mark took a little longer to make the move to Atlanta full time, but when he did, he lived about seven miles away. That's not a very long distance, but it was still a separation. We had been apart a lot over the course of several months, and when he came back into my life on a regular basis, it wasn't quite the same for him.

He was used to being around family, and so he didn't have a lot of guy friends to hang out with. He was used to doing everything with family. So he just didn't make friends as quickly as I did, and I was probably not as understanding as I should have been. Mark was out of sorts, and the first cracks in our relationship started to show up.

I had lived all over, moving constantly, so I was very adaptable. Mark was the opposite. He'd moved once in his life, when he got married, and that was two blocks away from his parents' house.

On top of that, Brenda was really starting to become a problem, and Mark resented all of the time I spent with her, trying to save her from herself.

And he was right, though it took me some time to come to that conclusion. At some point, people are either going to rise up and take responsibility for themselves or sink past the point that you can help them, and Brenda was nearing that place.

So Mark had left the only home he'd ever known, where his wife died, where his sons still lived, and moved to Atlanta where he had to share me with an outrageous drunk who caused problems wherever she went and who he really didn't like very much.

It was hard.

Brenda was one of my best friends, but after she inherited some money a couple of years before, she quit working and started partying full time. She hooked up with the wrong kind of men who took advantage of her, she drank too much and did too many drugs, and eventually she fell down the stairs when she was drunk, and suffered brain damage. After that, her behavior was even worse. Brenda just had a very destructive personality. It was difficult for me not to help her, and she became source of a lot of conflict between Mark and me.

Plus, Mark might come over on a Friday night, and I would be helping Jaimon with his homework, or something. So it was all pretty tough on Mark. I was becoming more independent, and he was becoming more dependent.

Something had to give.

We started to argue, which we had never really done, and it was mostly silly. He wanted me to come to his place more often, and I wanted him to come to my house, stuff like that. I even used the neighbors as an excuse.

"I came over three times in a row," Mark would complain.

"But you don't live across the street from Mrs. Chin's dumplings!" I answered.

She was a really good cook.

In my defense, there were many times after the move that I was sick, and Jaimon would come over and walk the dog, his parents would help clean my house, and Mrs. Chin would cook for me. Why would I want to leave all that?

I actually had a pretty rough time when I developed paraparesis, which is a weakness in the legs. They also call it drop-foot. Like when you see an elderly person who shuffles along instead of picking up their feet. I fell on my stairs and broke my ankle, and my neighbors really came through for me.

Especially Jaimon's parents. They were really protective of me after I practically saved them from a lynch mob after Jaimon's father somehow managed to ram his daughter's car into a transformer under the streetlight in front of their house, which took out the power to the entire neighborhood in the middle of the night. By the time the police showed up, everyone on the block was out in the street and very angry at poor Arjun, who barely spoke English and had just been trying to back the car into the driveway. But all the neighbors knew was that some idiot knocked out the lights.

I took the cops aside and explained it was an accident, and then crossed the street and smoothed things over with the neighbors. Jaimon's parents loved me after that. I took a volatile situation and just calmed things down.

I've always been good in circumstances like that. Talking to people, working out solutions. It also helped that I knew the chief of police and the mayor.

Whenever I move to a new city, I always get to know the people in charge. Within a week of moving in, I go to the local church and I introduce myself around as someone with a background in fundraising and I offer my help if it's needed, and Roswell was no exception.

So while things were pretty settled for me, it wasn't the same for Mark.

It was also around that time that Joey got even sicker, and that was what led to our breakup.

Joey was very ill, and it affected his bodily functions.

Mark had finally closed on his house, and he'd flown his son Matthew down for the occasion. He wanted his first night as the owner to be special, so he asked me to stay the night with him there, too.

"What about Joey?"

"Jaimon can watch him."

Well, that was out of the question. Jaimon would have been okay with that, of course, but I wasn't. My dog of many years was very ill, and he was a mess. No way was I going to foist him off on someone else.

"I can't leave Joey," I said. "I won't."

We finally decided I would just bring the dog with me, and it was a disaster.

Aside from it being his first night in the house, Mark was also officially starting work the next day at his new office, so there was a lot going on for him. I should have realized it was all too much, but Mark really wanted me to be with him. And he really seemed to be trying with me, to adjust to all of these changes.

Joey woke us up at three in the morning, moaning, and when we turned on the lights there was bloody diarrhea all over Mark's brand new carpeting, which was white, of course. It was everywhere. In the bedroom, the den, it looked as if Joey had purposely gone through every open door in the house. It was awful.

Worse than any of that, of course, was the fact that I could tell Joey was dying.

Mark freaked out.

"I have to take Joey to the hospital," I said.

"What about this mess?"

I just looked at him. "I have to take care of Joey!"

And that's what I did. I wrapped that fifty-pound dog in a sheet and carried him downstairs as Mark and his son just watched in silence. I didn't even know where I was going, I just put my emergency flashers on and drove around until I found a cop, who led the way to an emergency animal hospital.

I stayed with Joey all night, and in the morning there was a brief glimmer of hope that he would be okay. So I went home, got cleaned up, and went back to Mark's house to see if I could do something about the mess.

Matthew was grossed out, Mark was furious, and we had another argument over who was going to use the shop-vac.

"It's my dog, I'll clean it up," I said.

"It's my shop-vac," he said, and proceeded to try and clean things up.

And that's when I snapped. First of all, he let his girlfriend leave the house in the middle of the night wearing nothing but a long dress shirt, knowing full well I had no idea where to go, and second, he knew how much Joey meant to me.

Carpet could be replaced. Joey could not.

We had a terrible fight right in front of his son, and I left. We broke up in an awful way. I said the words, and he said fine. It was another horrible night.

To Matthew's credit, he came to see me at the hospital the next day and tried to smooth things over. He was pretty even-handed about it.

But I was done. If he didn't love me enough to care about Joey, then I really didn't want him in my life anymore. In the meantime, Joey lived to fight another day. The doctor got him stabilized and I brought him home, and Jaimon and his parents helped me take care of him.

Mark called to apologize a few days later, and we both had a good cry and decided to try again. But I was really raw.

I insisted on paying to replace Mark's carpet, because it just could not be cleaned, and the two of us kind of tip-toed around each other, trying to get past the whole ugly incident. He was still worried about the dog, but I wouldn't hear about it. It's like when your kid is sick, you don't worry about the mess, you just want him to get better. But when it's someone else's kid, that's another story.

"I want you to be here more," he said. "This is my house, but I want it to be your house, too."

"Mark, I'm trying," I answered.

"You're not trying hard enough."

That got to me. He was right, I had been mostly concerned with myself, and there was probably a lot more that I could do. So I resolved to meet him halfway, but it was still a tense time. A lot had been said and done, and it was going to take a while to heal.

But we tried.

Then one night, it all came to an end, again.

I was two hours late coming over because traffic was really bad and I had been across town. I opened the door with my key, went inside, and Mark got off the couch, ready to confront me. I guess he'd been sitting there, fuming.

I tried to explain, but he wasn't buying anything I had to say.

"It's all about you, Carol. You think you can just come over whenever you want and everything will be fine."

"Don't be like that," I said, and I reached for him.

That's when he pushed my hand away and told me he didn't want me there.

I left immediately.

Within a couple of days, Mark knew I was beyond mad and I think he realized what he'd done. He called and called, but I refused to talk to him. He called Jaimon, Mrs. Chin, anybody he could think of, but I wouldn't see him or speak to him.

I found out later that he was keeping tabs on me, because back in the AOL days you could see if other people were online, and since we had met on Match.com, he was watching my profile there, too, to see if I had anything going on there.

Which of course, I did.

I met this really good-looking guy named Gino on the site, and we started dating. He traveled a lot and it wasn't serious, but he was fun to hang around with. He was a rebound guy.

That's when Mark went into high gear. He called my sisters and anybody else he could think of, asking about me and what he could do to get me back, that kind of thing. I have to admit I liked the thought of him out there, wondering about me.

Then one night he finally called me, and he was crying. I had never heard him like that.

"I know what I did," he said. "I know why that bothered you so much when I pushed you. I'd give anything to take it back, but I can't."

"Okay."

"I love you, Carol. I miss you so much. Please let me see you."

"Mark, it's not a good day," I said, and it really wasn't. "I'm not feeling well."

"Just let me bring you some soup, then," he said. "Please?"

I said okay. I really wasn't up to arguing, and soup did sound pretty good. The guy knew what I liked. Plus, I had no makeup on and hadn't bathed for two days, so if he wasn't bothered by any of that, that would definitely be a point in his favor.

He wasn't bothered.

The soup was wonderful, and he really worked to soften me up. He had found out from my sister that I was going to Rome with her in a few weeks, so he bought me a travel book and some lovely picture frames (one of which had a picture of us in it – nice move, honey), and I agreed to go out to dinner.

He asked me if I had been seeing anyone, and I answered truthfully, especially since I knew that he already knew.

"Is it serious?" He asked.

"That's not really any of your business, now is it?" I asked, and to his credit he didn't push the issue. I could tell he really wanted to, though, which was another couple of points in his favor. It was obvious that he cared who I was seeing, but he knew better than to get pushy with me about it.

When we went to the restaurant, the hostess greeted me warmly, said hello to Mark, and then blurted out, "So, you're not seeing Gino, anymore?"

It was pretty awkward, but it turned out to be the best thing she could have said.

I could feel Mark stiffen and flush with embarrassment, so I pulled his arm close and answered, "No, this is my real boyfriend."

I knew he would love hearing that, and it was a nice way for me to tell him where I stood without having a big discussion about it. It cleared the decks for us, you might say.

We had a wonderful dinner, and we've been together ever since.

20

Letting Go

ARK INSISTED THAT I NOT BOARD JOEY, but allow him to take care of the dog while I was in Italy with my sister Janet, which I thought was pretty amazing. Joey, of course, had been right in the middle of our first terrible fight when he bled all over Mark's new house, and the fact that Mark genuinely wanted to take care of him while I was gone really meant something to me. By this time, Joey literally had to be wiped like a baby, but Mark didn't care. He knew that Joey was important to me, and that meant he was important to Mark, as well.

Wiping my dog's ass. That's what I call over and above the call of duty. It was such a relief to know that Joey would be well cared for while I was gone.

My sister Janet, on the other hand, turned out to be quite a handful on our trip

I made all the arrangements since I was used to that sort of thing and we wanted to save money, and we left for our trip to Rome to celebrate my 50th birthday as happy as clams.

Janet had a secret, however, and that secret would have a pretty big impact on our trip.

What my sister had decided not to tell me was that she'd had a mini-stroke not long before we left! Imagine that. She didn't think that was something she might want to mention to me.

I'm sure she thought I would have canceled the trip, and she would have been right. At least I would have canceled it for her. That was a really dangerous thing to do, traveling to Europe right after having a stroke, but I guess she just really wanted to go. The thing was, my health was always on the verge of causing a problem. If I had an attack while I was overseas, I wanted to be with someone who could help me, not someone who was liable to have a stroke.

Janet had had a mini-stroke years before, and this was the second one. Who knew what might happen if she had a third?

But what I didn't know didn't freak me out, and so we landed in Rome extremely excited to see the city. Neither of us had ever been there, and it's really an amazing place. I'd spent hours looking through tour books to figure out what we'd be doing each day during the ten days of our trip.

Things did not start off so great, and it had nothing to do with our health.

The cab driver took us to our hotel, which was located in what looked like a not-so-nice area, otherwise known as a ghetto, and since neither one of us wanted to stay in a room with bars on the windows, we checked out the next morning and went looking for another hotel.

It's really something how the pictures in the tour books don't always tell the whole story.

The next day we looked at seventeen places before we were finally satisfied, but it was actually a nice way to introduce ourselves to the city. Everywhere you looked, there was something interesting to see, whether it was the architecture or the statues or the people. Rome is just an incredibly vibrant city.

After we finally got settled, of course we went sightseeing, and we had a lovely day. That night we went for cocktails at the top of the famous Spanish Steps, which was fabulous. We were laughing and making plans for my birthday, and generally having a great time.

That's when something started to go wrong with my sister.

"Do you see that guy?" She asked, pointing to a handsome young Italian walking toward the top of the steps.

I raised my glass. "Yes, I do."

Then Janet said, "I see two of him."

"That's it," I said, laughing. "No more drinks for you."

Although I have to admit, two of that guy would have been very interesting.

We left and walked down the steps, enjoying the cool night air, but when we got about halfway down, Janet suddenly collapsed and tumbled down the next several steps.

"Oh, my God, Janet!" I screamed, and ran to her. I knelt beside her and turned her face towards mine. She'd hit her head and was bleeding all over the place. She wasn't responding to my screams, either. Janet was unconscious.

Obviously you can't get an ambulance up the Spanish Steps, so I managed to pick her up and half-drag, half-carry my sister to the bottom. I was frantic by this time, screaming for help, and a hot dog vendor finally took pity on me and told me where to go for a cab. A lot of people just ignored us as if they saw two bloody women every night or something.

Janet finally regained consciousness, but she went in and out, so basically she would lean on me and we'd walk for a while, and then she'd pass out again and I'd drag her. I still didn't know that she'd just had a stroke, but I was pretty sure I was about to have a heart attack.

We finally made it back to the hotel, and Janet took one look in the mirror at her bloody face and nearly passed out again. It was awful. She also wasn't making a lot of sense when I asked her what the hell happened, so I called my sister Barbara back in the states. It was Barbara who told me Janet had recently had a stroke.

I couldn't believe these sisters of mine not telling me this!

"You knew she had a stroke and you didn't tell me?" I screamed.

"Carol, you need to get her to a hospital."

A woman at the hotel gave us a pill for Janet to take, which made her feel a lot better, and she started talking about how she didn't want to go to the hospital, but after my conversation with Barbara, I wasn't going to take any chances.

We took a cab to the hospital, and wouldn't you know it? The place was a madhouse, with protesters and strikers picketing outside and barely a place to squeeze through to get to the entrance. It had been hard to find a cab, so I wasn't sure if it was a taxi strike or a hospital worker strike or a combination, but I managed to push my way through the crowd and get her into the hospital.

This was all really scary, of course. I was in a foreign county and it seemed like my sister could die at any moment.

They kept her overnight and gave her an MRI the next day, but basically all they could do was put her on an aspirin regimen and tell her not to get on a plane again for at least four days.

Four days? I wanted to jump on a plane that night!

Janet was happy about the delay because she was determined to see Rome, so we spent the next four days sightseeing, with me on pins and needles waiting for my sister to keel over, and Janet having a wonderful time. I'm amazed that all the stress didn't bring on an attack, but I did pretty well, all things considered.

Happy birthday to me!

We did have a pretty good time in spite of all the craziness, which I suppose is pretty much par for the course when it comes to my family. If there's a moment of peace and quiet, one of us will always find a way to liven things up a little.

It kind of reminded me of the time my mother came into some money from an inheritance, and she and I went to France together. While there was no medical emergency like during my trip to Rome, my mother kept things pretty interesting. It was before I had Ryan and we acted more like girlfriends than a mother and daughter, giggling and laughing our way across Paris.

Once she carried off an entire wheel of cheese that was meant for the whole table full of people, thinking it was meant for her since the waiter had placed it closest to where she was sitting. Scooping up that big wheel of cheese was just like taking home the leftovers to my mother.

She actually put the whole thing in her purse as we were leaving, while the other diners looked at us like we were nuts. Neither of us really knew what we were doing.

We were halfway down the street before the waiter realized what she'd done and stepped out onto the sidewalk, screaming something about fromage, but my mother just kept walking.

"I don't understand French," she said.

At that point I think we both understood what was happening, but I wasn't about to suggest to my mother that we go back, at that point.

At least she left a nice tip.

Mom carried that smelly hunk of cheese all the way back to New York, too.

"What, am I going to waste it?" She said.

My mother. If she was going to go to all the trouble of stealing an enormous hunk of cheese and lugging it all over Paris, she wasn't about to let any of it go to waste.

Janet and I made it back from Rome in one piece, and not long after that I had to put Joey down, which, as I've mentioned, was a very traumatic event. Aside from Ryan, Joey had been the one constant in my life for many years, and it was really hard to let him go.

In retrospect, it made me very happy that Mark had taken care of him while I was away. He was there with me when we put Joey down, too.

A few months later, my dear friend Brenda, whose alcoholism had been slowly but steadily destroying her life, had a terrible fall while she was drunk, and suffered a traumatic brain injury.

It was all incredibly sad. Brenda had helped me a lot when I moved down to Atlanta, but once I got there I began to see that she was a lost soul. Brenda was one of those people who always spent more than she made, always had the best clothes and a fancy car, basically living on the edge. After she inherited half a million dollars from her father, things really went downhill for her. She retired and just let loose with bad men and bad decisions, and nothing I did could keep her from her terrible slide.

She didn't actually inherit the money, but she guilted her step-mother into giving her half the proceeds from the sale of her father's condo in Newport Beach. Her father had known she was an alcoholic and couldn't handle money, but her stepmom acquiesced, hoping the money would help provide a better life for her.

It was a noble gesture, but Brenda's father was right. It was a tragic mistake.

When she was working, Brenda had a reason to hold herself together, and she always looked like a million dollars, very well put together. She was a functional alcoholic, and even though we were close, I had no idea of the extent of her problem.

Once she decided to retire, she began her downward spiral.

With no place to go every day, Brenda was a disaster waiting to happen. As they say, the Devil finds work for idle hands. Many times I would have to go over and buy her groceries and clean her up because she had nothing in her house but booze and had peed all over herself. It was really disgusting, just a terrible situation.

Several hospital and rehab stays didn't help, and when she fell, she fell hard. Literally. She stumbled down the stairs of her townhouse after a fishy incident with an electrician at ten o'clock at night, and was in an induced coma for several days after while the doctors waited for the swelling in her brain to go down.

The night of the accident, the electrician managed to find her Aunt Sandy's number in Brenda's cell phone and call her. "She's hurt real bad," he said. "I called 911, but I have to go."

He hung up, left the phone next to Brenda, who'd hit the stairs so hard her brain was exposed, and left the door open for the paramedics.

Aunt Sandy lived two hours away. She later received a call from the electrician, who inquired how Brenda was and then asked to be paid for whatever electrical work he'd been doing at her townhouse at ten o'clock on a Saturday night. He said he didn't know anything about the cocaine in her system.

After her injury, I had to step in and help Sandy sell Brenda's townhouse and most of her belongings because she wasn't able to take care of herself at all.

We set up a trust with the money, got her into a group home, but even then she was a mess. She would leave in the middle of the night, hail a cab, and go to the liquor store or some club in her nightgown. It was terrible. She was in and out of nursing homes and group homes, always getting kicked out for sneaking booze in her room or something.

It turned out she had had electric shock therapy as a child, and developed multiple personality disorder, something I never knew. Her mother died of alcoholism when she was fourteen, Brenda had given up her only child for adoption when she was sixteen, also things I never knew. There was really just a lot wrong in her life from the time she was young, and she never really got past it.

I went into a deep depression after all this happened. We were like sisters, and I knew I was losing her. I was fatigued all the time from dealing with her. She just wore me out, and her Aunt Sandy, too.

Those were some pretty tough times.

We got Brenda in and out of various places, and finally we found a very nice group home run by a wonderful woman named Ann, and that's where she is today. I haven't seen Brenda in two years, and will probably never see her again. The last time I went to visit her, she got very belligerent and actually spit at me and hit me with her walker.

I cried a lot after that, and talked to my mother about what I should do. My mom had truly loved Brenda because we had been so close, but my mother is also one touch cookie.

"You have to let her go, Carol," she told me, and I knew it was true. My mother always had a knack for the simple, hard truths, and that was Brenda's and mine. I had to let her go. Brenda had finally taken everything out of me, and I just didn't have anything else to give, anymore. Even though I have an incurable disease, I still dread the day I get a call that Brenda has passed. She's only fifty-eight, but it seems as if her life is over.

I wish I didn't feel that way.

I keep track of her through Ann, as does her Aunt Sandy, who also had finally had enough.

Brenda just wore the two of us out, I guess.

I think one of the reasons I had to stop seeing her was because my own hold on things can be so tenuous. I'm very blessed, with wonderful parents who are still alive, a terrific son, and a loving husband. I have all the things Brenda never had, but I know that it could all come to an end at any time. Living with MS makes you appreciate every moment, but it also is a constant reminder of how fragile life really is.

I guess when it comes down to it, Brenda just scared me. I looked into her vacant eyes and saw myself. There but for the grace of God, and all that.

I pray for Brenda and keep in touch with Sandy and Ann, but that's all I can do for her now. I keep myself busy volunteering for others like her, though, people on the fringes, people for whom I can still make a difference. Sometimes it's easier to help a stranger than someone you know, but once you help someone, you're not a stranger any longer, so I guess it all kind of evens out.

I don't know what the future holds for Brenda, or for myself. I just know that life is a beautiful gift from God, everything happens for a reason, and we all just do what we can while we're here.

21

Helping Hands

EVEN THOUGH MY FAMILY ALWAYS STRUGGLED financially when I was growing up, a lot of relatives on my mother's side actually had accumulated a lot of holdings over the years that were held within a large trust, of which my mom was one of forty-two principals. The trust never really sold off much of anything until a few years ago, when they sold the Weather Channel.

So my mother, relatively late in life, came into quite a bit of money.

My mother's father had been a heavy drinker and gone from job to job, never quite able to succeed at any one thing, but his brothers and sisters were all business people who were very smart with their investments, the type of people who lived off the interest without touching the principle.

The money did not change my mother at all. She bought a nice little condo near the beach and a car, but that's about it. She's never been an extravagant person. She set up trusts for her grandchildren and took care of some things for my siblings and me, but she's just not the type to buy jewelry or fur coats or anything like that. Not for herself. She couldn't care less about the trappings of wealth.

The biggest thing she did was set up a charitable foundation, which I help run, which means that we're able to provide grants every year to people and organizations that help people in need. This is something she cares a great deal about, as do I.

Since I can no longer work full time, the foundation provides a way for me to stay active. I volunteer as much as I'm able, doing my part to help people going through hard times, which is very rewarding. Having been through a lot of tough times myself, I can relate to what a little helping hand can mean when you're down. I also help decide where the money goes.

Because of the trust, Mark and I needed a prenuptial agreement the size of a small city phone book before we got married, which is pretty ironic considering my poor childhood. I'm still surprised sometimes at how things turned out. Mark was fine with that, of course. He had his own assets, anyway, so a prenuptial agreement was both necessary and pragmatic.

Besides, I'd already been married once and lost almost everything, so I was looking at another marriage slightly less dewy-eyed this time around.

Like my mother, my lifestyle didn't really change all that much, either. Like her, I bought a nicer car and paid off my townhouse, and I can afford to take a couple of vacations a year, which is also nice, but overall, I don't really need much to make me happy. My mother and I are similar in that sense. We both like to give back and help other people, and now that we can, it's been a blessing.

The principals of my mom's foundation are just the five kids, myself and my brother and sisters, and we meet a couple of times a year to go over things and discuss worthy organizations, and then the rest of the year I work directly with our non-profit to hand out money to those good causes, in particular local charities. We support MS, of course, as well as organizations that help people with mental health issues. My sister Janet supports the local chapter of NAMI, the National Alliance on Mental Illness, and we donate to breast cancer research and treatment, food pantries, all kinds of things. My sister Joanne has a passion for music-based programs; we really spread it around.

I volunteer with Home Stretch, as I've mentioned, which is a terrific organization that helps people going through hard times get back on their feet. I do as much for them as I can aside from the grants, assisting the social workers with outreach and support and even answering phones if they need me to. I even mentor families, making sure they know they can reach out to me if there are problems. Basically, I'm a sympathetic ear to the families we place in our twenty-eight housing units, all duplexes located in a suburban cul-de-sac.

We have weekly classes taught by volunteers that teach money management and other important life skills, and each family gets a whole team of support, with an accountant, a social worker, and a family mentor, which is what I do. These families know not only that someone cares, but that someone is responsible, just like we expect them to be accountable. It's an amazing organization.

Our placements are all working class poor who just need a hand up. For whatever reason, they've either been thrown out of their apartment or lost their mortgage, and they're in a bad place. It's a moment in time that they could either be lost, or with a little help, get back on their feet and become productive citizens again. Maybe they've made some bad decisions, but they can prosper with a little help and guidance.

Home Stretch also gets money from the United Way and a lot of support from a local Presbyterian Church in the form of donations and volunteers. Whenever I'm physically able, I do whatever they need me to do, and of course, fund raising is right up my alley, so I help with those events, too.

It's wonderfully fulfilling work for me.

I remember one girl in particular who really touched my heart. Her name was Erica and she had two children with two different men, neither of whom was providing any support. Her family had pretty much given up on her because of some bad decisions she'd made, but she was a very smart girl. She worked as a certified nursing assistant during the day and took online courses at night to become an RN, so I could see that she was really trying to better her lot in life.

However, a certified nursing assistant only paid ten dollars an hour, which was just not enough to support her and two children, so I helped her get a job with UPS, which had good benefits and insurance and paid a lot more. She struggled with depression sometimes, and who wouldn't in that situation, but she didn't want to take any medication because she'd previously had a problem with drugs.

We finally convinced her that an anti-depressant could help, and after that she really thrived. Today she's an LVN, getting married to a really nice guy, and they're buying a house together. She was one of our real success stories.

There was another woman who really touched me, Susan, a mother of four from Texas who I met through my work with Berlex Labs. She'd been diagnosed with MS and had to use a wheelchair. She and her husband had always had money issues, but they'd managed to get by until her husband also lost his job.

In spite of all of these troubles, she always had an amazingly positive attitude. It was inspiring just to talk to her, really. She reminded me of what I'd gone through, all alone and doing her own research, struggling to find a way to a better life. She found me online and came to one of my talks, and I ended up getting Berlex Labs to hire her as a speaker. She flew all over the country sharing her story, and later even set up a social network for people with MS with a woman she met at one of her talks, with seed money from Annette Funicello, the well-known actress and former Mouseketeer.

Now Susan works with the National MS Society on issues with Medicare reform and the Affordable Care Act, so she's really come a long way from when we first met. It's amazing to think about many lives she's affected, and that I played a small part in helping her accomplish that.

This is really emblematic of my mother's legacy. She has inspired her children to join her in her charity, and each of us, in our own way, is trying to pay it forward however we can.

My mother also likes her grandchildren to be involved with the foundation as much as possible, if they want, because she wants them to feel the same way about giving back that she does, just like her own kids. The money we help her give away through her foundation is the money we would have otherwise inherited, so as she says, in that way only my mother can, "It's your money. Give it away!"

She also set up a medical trust for us, so it's also very comforting to know that my family's medical expenses are not something I have to worry about, anymore. Especially since, between me and Ryan, there's always something going on there.

For example, just before Mark and I got married, Ryan had to have an operation on his esophagus. He'd been born with a problem in that area which had always caused him problems, but the doctors promised always told me he would eventually grow out of it, acid reflux notwithstanding.

I'll never forget the first time I went to visit him in college. Most parents in that circumstance are on the lookout for empty liquor bottles, but what I found were a bunch of Maalox bottles all over his truck.

So around the time I had decided to marry Mark, Ryan transferred to the University of North Texas in Denton, about thirty miles north of Dallas. He was really having a lot of pain around that time due to acid reflux, sometimes even going to the emergency room. Eventually a doctor did x-rays and told us that the muscles around his esophagus had practically deteriorated over the years, which was causing all the problems.

The surgeon told us that he would have to basically move his stomach and spleen and repair the damage, but it was actually a pretty simple operation, nothing to be too concerned about.

Not.

I flew to Dallas for the operation, and took Ryan back to my hotel about forty minutes away from the hospital as soon as he was released, which was only three hours after the surgery. They told me everything would be fine, and everything was fine until the anesthetic wore off, and then things wee terrible.

Ryan was in absolute agony. I was calling the ER and the doctors and anyone else I could think of, trying to figure out what to do. Since I didn't know anyone around there, it was very scary. It's always easier to deal with a crisis in familiar surroundings.

All of his insides had been shifted around, and Ryan was in terrible pain, literally screaming at times because it hurt so badly. They sent him off with antibiotics but no pain medication!

This is one of my pet peeves with health care. So many times a simple lack of communication causes even more suffering, and it's unnecessary. Just telling a patient what to expect can make such a difference to people when they're sick, and so often, no one bothers to do that. In this case, my son's insides were tight and needed time to loosen a bit and "settle," but no one told us that.

And, of course, no one told us about the excruciating pain.

The doctor finally called in a prescription for morphine pills the next morning, which meant Ryan suffered the entire night. Which meant we both suffered. There's nothing worse than the sound of your child hurting. It was awful.

I couldn't leave him for a minute, so one of his friends picked up the prescription for us. Meanwhile, I called his grandmother, Edith, who still lived in Texas, so she could try and locate his father to see if he could help, because it was obvious that my week-long stay was probably not going to be enough. The doctors said the surgery would be no big deal, so how could I know?

As far as I was concerned, Cody really should have been there, anyway.

Ryan's food had to be pureed, of course, so his friend Giuseppe helped out by bringing soup over to the hotel twice a day. He worked at a restaurant, which was great. The hotel was also very nice about accommodating us as best they could. Meanwhile, I was really ex-ing for my ex-husband to provide a little support.

ₚₒᵢₙt we ran out of antiseptic ointment for his incision, and since Ryan seemed to be doing a little better, I decided I could go down the street to the pharmacy and pick it up. I stopped and told the desk clerk what was going on, and he promised to keep tabs on Ryan while I was gone.

He probably should have kept an eye on me, as well, because when I opened the door to my son's truck, a bottle of Lone Star Beer fell out onto the pavement and exploded in the hundred-degree heat, sending a shard of glass into my leg and opening up a three inch flap of skin that looked like the white flag of surrender at the Alamo.

Okay, I know they never surrendered at the Alamo, but at that moment I wasn't real fond of the great state of Texas or its beer or its heat wave.

Blood was gushing out of my leg as I hobbled back into the hotel, leaving a gory trail across the lobby like something out of the Texas Chain Saw Massacre. People surrounded me with towels and questions, and all I could think of was that I'd promised my son I'd be right back and now look what happened.

I asked the clerk if someone could get the prescription for me, and he said of course, but I'm sure what he really wanted was for me to stop bleeding all over the lobby. I had dealt with plenty of stressed out guests during my time in the hotel business, but I'm not sure I ever had someone like me at that moment.

Finally, I managed to get back up to the room, and Ryan immediately told me to go to the hospital. He was in pain and in and out of consciousness, but even he could tell I was in bad shape.

"I can't leave you here, Ryan."

"Mom-"

"I'm not leaving you here by yourself!"

Ryan called Mark to complain about his stubborn mother, and then Mark tried to convince me to go get stitched up. Between the two of them and the fact I couldn't stop the bleeding even with towels and pillowcases, I finally agreed. Thank God there was an ER only a couple of blocks away.

I was still bleeding when I got there, and thought I lucked out because the place was empty. I told the nurse that I had to get back to my son as soon as possible, and just as she was saying that shouldn't be a problem, the doors burst open and the place goes into a typical emergency room, full-blown organized chaos.

There had apparently been a really bad car accident nearby and now my injury was dropping fast on their list of priorities.

I was hysterical. I wanted to be there when Ryan took the morphine every three hours, since when a person is doped up, mistakes can be made. I called another friend of Ryan's who worked in a pharmacy, and he not only went over to see Ryan to give him his meds, he then came to see me in the emergency room and helped expedite my treatment.

Ryan has some wonderful friends, let me tell you. I don't know what I would have done without them. He's like me; he makes friends wherever he goes. Ryan's just a wonderful guy with some really wonderful friends.

Eight hours later, I finally made it back to the hotel, and Giuseppe had brought over some more food and even a bottle of wine. I was an absolute mess. Exhausted, sore, and worried about Ryan.

Giuseppe took one look at me and said, "If you didn't have bad luck, you'd have no luck at all."

It was tempting to agree with him, but I knew that just by being there, Giuseppe had actually proved himself wrong. As bad as everything got, and it had been pretty crazy, the good Lord was watching over me, as He had so many times before.

I was still waiting for Cody, of course, who was driving in from an Oklahoma oil field, and by the time he got there, I was ready to collapse. He started to give me some shit about how I should've known more about what could happen, but I shut him right down. He'd literally been a three-hour drive from Ryan the entire time and I'd flown in from Georgia, and he had the nerve to say something like that to me after the day I'd had?

"You should've been here from the get go," I said.

To his credit, he knew I was right and apologized, and I decided to give him a pass. I know he was just concerned for his son, the same as I was.

I went into the adjoining suite after going over all the instructions with Cody, and then finally got some rest.

For the next week, Ryan's dad carried him to the bathroom, cleaned his wound, bathed him, and gave him his pain pills, with me right there making sure everything was okay. After that, Ryan was able to go back to his apartment, where Cody stayed another week. It was a small place and I was comfortable that Cody would take care of things, so I flew back to Atlanta.

Never again will Ryan get acid reflux, but he has to take it easy. He can never throw up, for example, so he can't drink or overeat or even get sick, really, like with the flu, because nothing is coming back up once it goes down. It was a life changing experience for him, but he's handled it very well. He's become a very good cook, eats healthy, and takes care of himself. Every year he participates in the national MS 150, which is a hundred and fifty mile bike ride to raise money for multiple sclerosis, but of course, being that he's in Texas, their ride is actually a hundred and eighty miles, from Houston to Austin.

As they say, everything's bigger in Texas.

22

By the Seat of My Pants

AS I LOOK BACK OVER MY LIFE, I'M AMAZED at how things have worked out. As I said in the beginning, I'm a fighter, but there's no way I would have gotten this far without the good Lord's help and the help of a lot of His children.

My family has been right there with me every step of the way, and that is a blessing for which I will be eternally grateful. My parents, God love them, have been the best anyone could ask for, and the same for my brother and sisters. Mark and I are now settled and very happy, and of course my son Ryan has always been my rock. He is what I'm most proud of.

Knowing that whenever I leave this earth I will be leaving behind a little part of myself within that wonderful young man makes me very happy.

I've been thinking about that a lot as I've gone back through my memory to write this book. The generational thing. I feel like I'm passing the torch. Ryan is now engaged, and will be starting a family of his own, soon.

There are a lot of changes with my disease, too. I've been injecting interferon for many years now, and it has made my life immeasurably easier, but my white blood cells and liver enzymes have finally had enough of it.

The medication I've relied on for almost twenty years has now become toxic.

It's always something.

Back when I first started taking interferon, no one really knew anything except that it had been helpful in clinical trials, but of course the long-term effects were a big mystery in the treatment of MS. Now, a lot of other people like me who were there in the beginning have had to stop taking it.

In a lot of ways we were pioneers, and even though the future wasn't clear, I think it's safe to say that the future is never really clear for anyone. In a way, we're all just constantly finding our way, flying by the seat of our pants.

Fortunately, the FDA has just approved a new drug that I have recently begun taking, called Tecfidera. It's a pill, which is a lot better than the injections, and I have high hopes that it will help me continue to live a full life. It seems to have minimal side effects, so it's almost like a dream come true.

The only problem is the cost, which is so much more expensive than it needs to be. I have Medicare and a medical trust set up by my mother, so the price won't affect me, but so many others out there may not be able to afford it, which is a terrible shame.

The drug has been around for a long time as a treatment for psoriasis, and I'm sure no one paid five thousand dollars a month for it, then. The maker, Biogen, has a program for people who can't afford it and aren't otherwise covered under their insurance, but I know there will be a lot of people who fall through the cracks. There always are.

That's why I still volunteer with Homestretch. To try and help some of those people who would otherwise be forgotten or shoved aside in our society. A helping hand, since I have been so fortunate in my own life. I want to pay it forward as much as I possibly can for as long as I possibly can.

As I was finishing this book, my son Ryan proposed to his fiancée on a plane because he first met her on a plane, which I found darling, and one of the great joys of my life will be seeing my own grandchildren. That is something I would have never thought possible all those years ago when I was first diagnosed with MS.

Ryan himself was not supposed to be possible, but that was just the first of many times I decided to keep my own counsel and fly by the seat of my pants.

It has made all the difference.

Of course, I realize that grandchildren will sort of be up to Ryan and Valentina, but since my son will be the first person to read this, I thought I might as well give him another little nudge.

The bottom line is, I'm in a good place. I've tried to live the best life I could with what I had, and thanks to God, my son, my husband, and my family, it really has been a wonderful life.

And I have faith that the best is yet to come.

Made in the USA
Middletown, DE
09 August 2021